LEADING

A

LEARNING

ORGANIZATION

THE SCIENCE OF
WORKING WITH
OTHERS

CASEY REASON

Solution Tree | Press

a division of

Solution Tree

555 North Morton Street
Bloomington, IN 47404
800.733.6786 (toll free) / 812.336.7700
FAX: 812.336.7790

email: info@solution-tree.com
solution-tree.com

FSC
Mixed Sources
Product group from well-managed
forests and other controlled sources
Cert no. SW-COC-002283
www.fsc.org
© 1996 Forest Stewardship Council

Visit **go.solution-tree.com/leadership** to download resources in this book.

Printed in the United States of America

13 12 11 10   2 3 4 5

Library of Congress Cataloging-in-Publication Data

Reason, Casey
  Leading a learning organization : the science of working with others / Casey Reason.
      p. cm.
  Includes bibliographical references and index.
  ISBN 978-1-934009-57-4 (perfect bound) -- ISBN 978-1-935249-35-1 (library binding) 1. School management and organization--Psychological aspects. 2. Educational leadership--United States. 3. Learning. I. Title.
  LB2805.R36 2009
  371.2001'9--dc22
                          2009028280

Solution Tree
Jeffrey C. Jones, CEO & President

Solution Tree Press
President: Douglas M. Rife
Publisher: Robert D. Clouse
Director of Production: Gretchen Knapp
Managing Editor of Production: Caroline Wise
Senior Production Editor: Edward Levy
Proofreader: Elisabeth Abrams
Text Designer: Amy Shock

Cover Designer: Pamela Rude

Parents Janice and Tuffy, wife Lisa, sons Brice and Kiah,
you fill each space with love.

Acknowledgments

My wife, Lisa Reason, met Solution Tree president Jeff Jones in 2006 and convinced him to listen to her husband's five-minute elevator speech on learning leadership. Jeff's enthusiasm, kindness, and belief in me in the years that followed have been a great inspiration, and I owe him and my remarkably supportive, energetic, and loving wife a great deal of thanks in helping make this book possible.

Rick and Becky DuFour have also been very generous with their time, suggestions, and encouragement over the past few years while bringing my work forward. Their contribution is an inspiration and sets a higher standard for us all.

While working in the Detroit area as an assistant superintendent, I had the pleasure of working with Joyce Fouts, the executive director of the Galileo Leadership Consortium. Joyce is an incredibly passionate leader, advocate, and friend whose authenticity, enthusiasm, and genuine concern for others inspired me to understand teacher leadership in a way that wouldn't have been possible without her guidance. Thanks to Joyce, I also had the chance to spend extended periods of time with Bob Marzano, Linda Lambert, and Eric Jensen, which has shaped my perspectives in a profound way.

Mike Carmean was the superintendent who believed that I could lead one of the largest schools in the state of Ohio at age thirty. He let me lead, learn, make mistakes, and keep trying to make things better. His passion for students and his desire to make a difference were with me throughout. My doctoral advisor, Eugene T. W. Sanders, talked me into studying leadership and out of studying school finance. Thanks to Dr. Sanders, I found my life's work.

Robert Sornson is a writer, scholar, and friend who understands learning better than anyone I've met, and his wisdom and encouragement have helped me discover so much about this profession. Finally, in my company, I've received outstanding research and technical support from Brenna Burghardt, Shannon Gessner, Stephanie Grant, Mara Leahy, and Karen Tscherne. Thanks to each of you for your loyalty, friendship, and tireless support.

Solution Tree Press would like to thank the following reviewers:
Barbara J. Erwin
Clinical Associate Professor, School of Education
Indiana University
Bloomington, Indiana

Margaret Preston
Dean of Instruction
Waltrip High School
Houston, Texas

Arthur Stellar
Superintendent of Schools
Taunton School District
Taunton, Massachusetts

Robert Sylwester
Emeritus Professor of Education
University of Oregon
Portland, Oregon

Pat Wolfe
Educational Consultant
Napa, California

Table of Contents

About the Author

 Casey Reason has worked with hundreds of educational leaders from all over the world, from inner-city Phoenix to Auckland, New Zealand, on breakthrough strategies designed to improve performance and overcome resistance to change. At age thirty, Casey was named principal of Whitmer High School, one of the largest urban schools in Ohio. Using innovative leadership and reform strategies based on collaboration, the staff of Whitmer led an impressive turnaround in student achievement and behavior.

In addition to leadership consulting and research, he specializes in instructional design, and since 2003 has developed more than fifty graduate- and doctoral-level distance learning courses.

Casey's work has been featured in *Educational Leadership*, and he has been a national presenter numerous times with the National Association of Secondary School Principals, the Association for Supervision and Curriculum Development, the Southern Regional Education Board, and the University Council for Educational Administration.

Casey earned his PhD. in educational leadership from Bowling Green State University. He is president of Highpoint Learning, an Arizona-based consulting company he runs with his wife, Dr. Lisa Reason. The Reasons live with their twin sons, Brice and Kiah, in Scottsdale, Arizona.

Introduction

Deep, meaningful change in schools occurs when the sacred exchange between teachers and students is supported and nourished. That happens when the adults who come to work each day continuously strive to improve their individual and collective capacity to learn. By themselves, new schedules, teaching materials, and slogans will not generate change that lasts. Truly transcendent learning organizations are led by teacher leaders and principals dedicated to making thoughtful, strategic organizational learning a priority.

Many leadership books have used stories of model leaders to illustrate the path toward effectiveness; we've studied the habits and read about the successes of corporate leaders, coaches, and military heroes and have attempted to identify and harness their wisdom. Other books have taken the approach of offering theories and defining leadership practice. This text builds on both of these approaches by examining more closely the psychological and neurological factors that affect how we lead and how groups are most effectively led; it also identifies more precisely how we can stimulate the deepest levels of individual and team learning.

Advanced brain imaging techniques, unavailable before the year 2000, allow us to observe the brain in action and give us a new perspective on leading and learning. For example, we now know that it's almost impossible to retain new learning unless it's emotionally relevant (Shu-Shen, 2008). We know that, while the literature on leadership has focused for years on the importance of having and communicating a vision (Hallinger, 2003; Hallinger & Heck, 2002; Bass & Avolio, 1988), establishing a collective vision is a complex neurological process. We also know that stress and fear can stop learning in its tracks and that leaders who use fear are actually impoverishing the learning environment (Oathes & Ray, 2008).

By taking advantage of the implications of these new findings for organizational learning, we can move past the distraction, fear, and stress in our schools to stimulate deeper levels of growth and creativity.

Who Are the Leaders, Who Are the Led?

When you think about school leaders, do you visualize the principal? Certainly, an abundance of research has acknowledged the principal's role in shaping school culture (Gross, 2009; Belmonte & Cranston, 2009; Karakose, 2008). Principals are often in the best position to significantly change work patterns in ways that immediately and effectively diminish distraction and promote higher levels of learning. Principals can unleash the awesome and often untapped potential that is dormant in just about every school. If you are a principal, *Leading a Learning Organization* is for you.

This book is also written for another emerging leadership force in schools—teacher leaders. *Teacher leadership* is a term we love to use in our profession but often apply inappropriately. In some schools, sadly, teacher leadership is demonstrated by visibility in the principal's office, where highly effective, seasoned educators set aside decades of classroom experience to work on issues like budgets and dress codes. Teacher leaders do not deny the value of these functions, but they know that the most significant work in school goes on not in the principal's office but in the classroom. All the efforts of boards of education, superintendents, support staff, and parent organizations come to fruition in one form or another in the classroom. By shaping the human spirit and finding the untapped greatness in others, teacher leaders redefine their school, their community, and the world.

The Steep Slope of Change

After thirty-two years as a history teacher, Lonnie was promoted to principal. A self-described traditional leader, he felt that the best way to honor the past was to live in it. As forces of change emerged, Lonnie greeted them with outright rejection or else derailed their momentum with his fatiguing capacity to filibuster every meeting he attended. When innovators sought to address a 25 percent failure rate in ninth-grade math and science, Lonnie roared back with an oral history of decades of failed change efforts and poor central office and board level support. In classic style, he also blamed the students and parents. As teachers with new ideas updated their resumes, he held firm and was lionized by a small but politically powerful group of old teaching colleagues.

Lonnie did not last long as principal. Over the years, his band of time-capsule associates shrunk, and the world began to change around him. In 2002, he was at the foothills of the steep slope of change in our profession, which is forcing all of us to acknowledge that change is no longer something that we can choose to ignore—it's here, and here to stay!

While Lonnie tried to exert control by limiting the flow of information, teachers today open source their classroom challenges and get suggestions for innovations from colleagues all over the world. Complex social networks have emerged, allowing for the creation of creative alliances and expanded perspectives. While Lonnie attempted to filter and reinterpret information from the state or district, news now hits the iPhones of staff members even before the principal comes in from bus duty. Clearly, technology has opened the doors of access and created a dynamic that has changed schools forever. Rather than rage against this steep slope of change, we need to acquire an adroit understanding of individual and team learning and the steps we can take to enhance it.

Thoughtfully leading a learning organization in a highly integrated, technologically evolved culture will require new approaches and perspectives. While the establishment of professional learning communities is on the rise, the expectation of standardization has also been accelerated, creating a unique and challenging paradox (Giles & Hargreaves, 2006). This text is designed to give courageous learning leaders perspectives and approaches in meeting this challenge.

An Overview of *Leading a Learning Organization*

Chapter 1 discusses the importance of the emotional tenor of a learning organization and explores, through the concept of strategic emotional focus, the specific steps learning leaders can take to harness the power of emotion to support learning. Chapters 2 and 3 address the concepts of fear and stress, respectively, and their powerful effects on a school's emotional tenor. These chapters explain why schools gravitate toward these emotions, which do so much to hinder organizational learning, and introduce strategies for managing them.

Chapter 4 explores the ways we shape our experience into mental representations and what effect the prevalent mental representations in a school have on leaders' attempts to build a collective vision. Chapter 5 looks at how the questions we ask are determinative of the answers or outcomes we get and discusses how asking the right questions works in the context of learning leadership. Chapter 6 examines how what we have learned about memory has influenced our understanding of learning.

Chapter 7 discusses concrete steps we can take to deal with learning overload and the importance of defining learning priorities and making those priorities our focus. In chapter 8, we discuss the overall learning context and look at research regarding the ideal learning environment. In chapter 9, we address the mechanics of collaboration as it relates to learning.

Each chapter begins by presenting the core knowledge learning leaders should have about that topic and ends with corresponding strategies and solutions they can implement. Through consideration of these topics and solutions, the reader should emerge with a much deeper sense of what it takes to stimulate organizational learning in schools.

Visit **go.solution-tree.com/leadership** to download and print many of the tables and graphs in this book.

CHAPTER 1

Strategic Emotional Focus

Emotion is the driving force behind our work in schools. Schools that make a difference in a positive way are continually immersed in emotions like love, courage, and hope, while schools that are self-destructive are plagued with emotions like fear and anger. The emotional tenor of a school is up to those who work in it. Individual and collective emotional states can ebb and flow quite dramatically according to circumstances, but they also fluctuate mightily because of the choices people make.

You can probably relate to a time in your career when you came together with colleagues and were courageous, focused, strong, and effective. You may have thought to yourself, "Why can't it be this way more often?" In fact, it can. Over the last several years we have learned that, although emotions can't be programmed, where we place our focus and what actions we take have a significant impact on the emotional states we experience (Smallwood, Fitzgerald, Miles, & Phillips, 2009; Kaplan, Bradley, Luchman, & Haynes, 2009), and this, in turn, has significance for how school leaders bring about change.

In this chapter, we explore how to harness the power of emotion in order to dramatically improve organizational learning and bring a greater sense of satisfaction to the work we do. Rather than leave the emotional tenor of a school up to chance, we can intentionally promote a climate that is conducive to learning.

Keep in mind, however, that focusing on positive and empowering emotions is not a feel-good solution; all emotions have their place. Thoughtful school leaders won't make much progress by simply denying what they feel. Instead, they must monitor all the emotions they feel, work to keep certain emotional impulses in check, and focus their responses to issues and events in ways that are most effective.

Emotion has always inspired both profoundly helpful and incredibly destructive behaviors. Consider these words from two of the most influential voices of the twentieth century:

> I believe that unarmed truth and unconditional love
> will have the final word in reality.

> I use emotion for the many and reserve reason for
> the few.

The first quotation is from Dr. Martin Luther King, Jr., the second from Adolf Hitler. King is remembered as a champion of peace, love, and hope. While time fades our memories of his political and policy influence, we recall with vivid clarity the emotional tenor of his life's work. Hitler, of course, left behind a legacy of unprecedented destruction driven by fear and terror.

We don't have to wait for a transcendent leader like Dr. King to appear in order to successfully lead change. Every school has pockets of brightness inspired by profound emotions. A school labeled as failing may have teachers who refuse to believe their students fit that label. By overcoming their own feelings of discouragement, despair, and anger, they can inspire others with hope and determination.

Core Knowledge: Emotion

Even in professionally difficult and unpredictable times, learning leaders can emerge from the classroom or principal's office and strategically use empowering emotions to create a new climate in their schools. To do so, they will need to take advantage of the following core aspects of our knowledge about learning and emotion.

Emotion Is the Genesis of Learning

Neurologically speaking, learning is a sophisticated process in which the neurons in the brain become stimulated, bundle together, and create new configurations. The neuron-bundling process begins when the neurons are stimulated by our emotions (Gregory & Parry, 2006). Clearly, this has enormous implications for leading organizational learning. If learning is the door to deep and sustainable organizational change, then emotions are the key to that door.

Schools Devote Emotional Energy to What Is Relevant

Our attention goes to what is most relevant; if we are hungry and afraid, the brain won't allow us to focus on a good book or a great work of art. In fact, the brain never stops scanning its environment for threats to our safety and well-being (Larsen, 2000; Tice & Bratslavsky, 2000). This is why any group that someone has manipulated into feeling a great deal of fear will stay tuned and take some action.

However, we are not always engaged in a struggle for survival. We ascribe emotional relevance to other issues in our lives, based on our experience or cultural norms. A team of teachers that successfully implements a dropout prevention program takes this action to support struggling learners not out of fear but for a variety of other reasons, including a desire to interrupt generational patterns of dropping out.

Emotional First Impressions Are Key

An emotional first impression is the initial emotional and physiological response connected with any new learning or event (Levenson, 2003). A fly landing on someone's hand and flying away will be quickly forgotten because it is unimportant and the brain doesn't register any emotion associated with that event. Conversely, the birth of a child will stimulate extremely intense emotions that will stay with the parents forever.

Once these emotional first impressions are established, it is very hard to change them (Levenson, 2003). If you meet someone new and find out just before shaking that person's hand that he or she won the Nobel Peace Prize last year, your emotional sensors will kick in and shape your impression. On the other hand, if you found out that your new acquaintance had just been released from Rikers Island Prison in New York, you would have a very different first impression. In both cases, every subsequent interaction would most likely be conditioned by the emotional mindset established at that first meeting.

In schools, too, emotional first impressions direct learning. If the state mandates a new reading program for an elementary school under threat of a takeover, it's likely that the introduction of that program will be associated with fear and threat-related emotions. Five years later, the staff will probably still associate that reading program with those emotions. Imagine if the desire to change the reading program were generated instead by a team of teachers who courageously decided that they could do more. Instead of fear becoming the emotional first impression, they would associate the program with hope and enthusiasm. The same reading program implemented by the same teachers can carry completely different associations.

Your mother may have encouraged you to make a good first impression. Neurologists and thoughtful learning leaders now know that, scientifically speaking, your mother was right! Our first emotional impressions drive how we think, feel, and respond.

Emotion Is a Call to Action—But Not Just Any Action

Everyone feels emotions, but not everyone responds to them in the same way. The fear impulse may drive a teacher or principal to overreact, lash out, overeat, or all of the above. Others feel that same impulse and recognize it as a signal to reflect, plan, and prepare—and only afterward to act.

Poor performance on a state test could bring feelings of shock, disappointment, fear, and embarrassment. Rather than acknowledging these emotions in a direct and honest fashion, staff members might begin to blame each other, the students, or the community for this failure. As a team, they may know that the students would do much better if they could pull together and deal with the *cause* of their emotional response; instead they increase their frustration levels.

Another school might experience that same shock, disappointment, fear, and embarrassment and harness those emotional impulses to drive the desire to change, focusing on emotions like courage, love, and determination. Learning leaders understand that events drive the emotional first impression; thoughtful schools reflect on that first impression and carefully choose a productive course of action. They know that the ability to reflect on and manage our emotions thoughtfully leads to deeper learning and improved focus (Weisinger, 1998).

Muting Emotion Slows Progress

Emotions can inspire absurd and inappropriate responses. As many a poet has pointed out, love can drive the soberest among us to throw humility and caution to the wind, with dire consequences. This is why many school leaders are nervous about openly discussing the impact of emotion and why schools tend to *mute* their emotions—that is, reduce the intensity of emotions they are trying to avoid (Gross & Levenson, 1997). In order to drive profound levels of new learning, learning leaders should not deny or excessively mute emotional impulses. Instead, they must demonstrate the courage to bring emotion out in the open and use it to drive new learning and change.

Athletes know that muting emotion may keep them from being fully engaged during a practice or competition. School leaders must approach challenges in the same way. If staff meetings produce low levels of emotion, change the routine. If no one is moved by a particular challenge or goal, explore why this is the case, and evaluate what the group could do to make the challenges at hand more inspiring and engaging.

Some schools have silently decided that the negative emotions are so intense, it's better not to go near them at all. These schools have had so much bad news and pain that even when good news comes their way, they hesitate to bask in the richness of their good feelings for fear of making themselves vulnerable to disappointment and frustration. In almost every school, there are pockets of pride, courage, and passion that are being denied or muted out of fear and confusion. Teachers or principals who act as if they don't care are often passionate leaders who have been hurt or deeply disappointed at some point and have retreated to a state of muting their emotions to avoid feeling that kind of pain again.

However, suppressing emotion over a long period of time can have a negative impact on our health and even our longevity (Mate, 2004). Muting emotion can lead to reduced immune functioning, increased feelings of isolation, and diminished memory (Klein & Bratton, 2007; Seeman, 2001; Uchino, Cacioppo, & Kiekolt-Glaser, 1996).

Furthermore, living or working with someone who is constantly suppressing emotion can increase the stress levels of those around that person and even induce the same physical responses to suppression as those of the suppressor (Butler, Lee, & Gross, 2007; Butler et al., 2003). Suppressing emotion also renders us unable to develop the close and authentic relationships necessary to form a team or group (DePaulo & Kashy, 1998). The suppressor's lack of expressivity often results in reduced interpersonal connection and the inability to build rapport and affiliation (DePaulo & Kashy, 1998).

Suppression also creates alienation, a sense of inauthenticity, concerns about self-presentation and social acceptance, as well as an overall impression of disingenuousness (Gross & John, 2002). Ironically, rather than making bad feelings go away, muting emotion may actually increase negative emotional experiences such as disgust, anger, embarrassment, and sadness and decrease the level of positive experience (Harris, 2001; Richards & Gross, 1999, 2000; Gross & John, 2002).

Without being open to emotional intensity, we can't reach the outer limits of our abilities. Schools that do amazing things are led by teachers and principals who are not afraid to laugh, cry, grit their teeth, hope, and be disappointed.

Rumination Interrupts Learning

We tend to relive important life experiences in our minds. The process of reconstructing our memories, evaluating our experiences, and reevaluating our actions and the actions of others is part of the learning process. After helping a child break through a particular learning challenge, for example, we may go back over the steps we took in order to apply them to other students.

At times, however, we find ourselves overly transfixed on particular patterns of memory reconstruction, dwelling on a particular issue or event. Our reconstruction may then shape—and inappropriately reshape—the emotional relevance of that event or issue. This process is referred to as *rumination* (Nolen-Hoeksema, 1991).

Rumination is not confined to life-changing events. In the teachers' lounge, a group might discuss a decision the principal recently made, hypothesize irresponsibly regarding his intent, and project unlikely dire consequences. Repeated verbalizations like this lead to a kind of oversaturation of emotions (Zech, 2000). Soon, a benign decision has evolved into something sinister, and an avalanche of negative feelings emerges. If they are repeated often enough and with enough intensity, it becomes difficult to see the principal in any light other than the distorted one created by rumination.

Emotional Variety Supports Focus

The brain tends to keep us in one emotional state at a time (Gregory & Parry, 2006), and on a very basic level those emotions are either pleasant or unpleasant. A school staff may look at its second-grade reading scores and see that they are the lowest in the school's history. This might evoke an unpleasant emotional response. A staff that is not good at recognizing emotional variety may simply sense "unpleasant feeling" and begin to distract itself or ignore the impulse. Alternatively, staff members may resort to more easily accessible forms of emotional expression, such as fear and anger. However, a more informed school might reflect on the news, acknowledge the issues, and realize that the staff's feelings are related to the embarrassment and remorse they associate with the poor performance.

Members of a school staff that embrace emotional variety are thoughtful about what their emotional reactions mean, what lies beneath them, and what actions should be taken. They also recognize the subtle differences in what they are feeling and don't clump emotional reactions like disappointment and regret into broader generalized emotional reactions like anger and fear (Adolphs, Baron-Cohen, & Tranel, 2002; London, 1997; Rathi & Rastogi, 2008).

Schools that regularly experience a greater variety of emotions also don't waste time on emotional rumination. They know that determination, pride, and courage can be stimulated after feeling embarrassment, regret, or remorse. Emotional variety can flourish in a trusting environment where sharing emotion and feelings is accepted, rewarded, and encouraged (Panda, 2008; Anbu, 2008).

Emotional Sag Blocks the Response

Emotional sag refers to the tendency to retreat to emotional states that are easy, common, or immediately accessible—the opposite of emotional variety. Some schools will always find a reason to be angry. Due to the deliberate actions of a few, their emotional energies have been trained to flow in that direction—especially in the face of change. If staff members from this school won the lottery, they would angrily perseverate on the tax implications; their reflections on a trip to the beach would more than likely consist of frustrated recollections of sunburn and traffic!

Sagging emotions, either individually or as a group, keep us from taking action or responsibility. It is easier for a principal to get angry at teachers than to be embarrassed or regretful regarding his or her own inaction, miscalculations, and mistakes. Teachers might allow themselves to sag into an emotional reaction of anger toward each other or the principal instead of seizing a collective opportunity to address complex issues of systemic change and strategic improvement. Sagging emotions also allow us to avoid doing any real work while denying us the richness of professional fulfillment.

Perhaps sagging is the brain's attempt to give us relief when we're feeling fatigued or overwhelmed. We all know that it's easier to complain at the end of a long day in school than at eight in the morning, when we're brimming with energy and hope. However, if we get in the habit of constantly sagging our emotions, we'll never take advantage of the profound learning opportunities the issues at hand present.

Leaders Help Shape the Emotional Tenor

It is a mistake to assume that somehow a team of leaders can create a school culture that is always collectively grateful, courageous, and happy. However, as we have seen, groups who come together do tend to establish a collective, shared emotional tenor (Bosco, 2007; de Rivera, Kurrien, & Olsen, 2007; Yang & Mossholder, 2004).

Arguably, emotional tenor is always up for grabs. Two or three outrageously happy or angry teachers entering into the teachers' lounge can reshape the emotional climate of the whole school. In some schools, significant influencers emerge whose ability to intimidate is so great that avoiding their wrath becomes a predominant issue. School leaders who are too afraid to confront cruelty and sarcasm unwittingly support the presence of negative emotional states, while principals and prominent teacher leaders who publicly recognize acts of courage and kindness reinforce those emotions, inspiring more of the same. Every action a prominent school leader takes demonstrates his or her priorities and belief system.

Many school staffs believe that the principal is the main conduit to shaping the emotional tenor of the organization. School principals do make a number of important decisions that serve to reinforce the values and beliefs of the organization; a principal who isolates his or her teachers and works in a cruel and arbitrary manner can thwart what could have been decades of love and courageousness. Conversely, a principal who uses the power of his or her position to endorse more affirming emotional states can quickly turn around a toxic emotional culture. Interestingly, a number of spirit-driven, committed schools have been operating with deep levels of love and generosity for decades through the tenures of a number of principals with dramatically different leadership styles (Day, 2000; Kaliprasad, 2006). What this suggests is that teachers who work together for decades and establish complex social networks have a lot to say about the emotional tone of a school. In fact, a principal has very little chance to stop a school full of determined teachers dedicated to working in a climate driven by love, thoughtfulness, and compassionate commitment.

Who decides the emotional tenor of your school? You do. So does the person next to you. It's decided each day based on your actions and reflections and on the mental models you hold regarding your work and yourself.

Emotional Resilience and Abundance Empower Change

Emotional resilience refers to the capacity to bounce back and reframe experience in the face of difficult challenges or negative and disempowering emotional patterns (Freitas & Downey, 1998; Carver, 1998). Principals and teaching colleagues make mistakes, and at times they disappoint or turn us off completely. Sometimes a school meets a bump in the road and allows that bump to derail its progress for an entire term. How well does your school or team bounce back from disappointment?

Emotional abundance is the term used in this text to describe the capacity of schools to experience emotions with clarity and intensity. A lack of *emotional abundance* may keep staff from feeling really joyful and satisfied in the face of success. When times are good, those good feelings should be enthusiastically shared. Outrageously courageous teachers should be outrageously celebrated. These celebratory feelings can ignite the passion to do it all over again!

When you are able to reach higher highs, it is easier to be reflective at the low points and to conjure up the strength, strategy, and courage to move back to the place where a more empowering emotional tenor once again leads the way.

Solutions in Action: Strategic Emotional Focus

This section focuses on a five-step protocol called *strategic emotional focus* (SEF) for directly evaluating the impact of emotion in your school and determining the steps you can take to recalibrate your school's emotional focus.

I have used this process over the years as a companion to building-wide strategic planning sessions and in small departmental groups, sometimes of fewer than five, who wish to work more effectively together. Some groups struggle a bit when attempting to have an in-depth conversation regarding the topic of emotion. Choosing the right facilitator for this conversation is essential, and sometimes it is easier for someone from outside the organization to lead it. If anyone from within the organization takes the lead, it's important that he or she be a trusted member of the team.

Step One: Evaluating Common Emotional States

The first step of this process is to thoughtfully reflect on the most common emotional states experienced, shared, and nurtured in your school. Since we tend to have a rather limited view of emotions, this text provides a tool to facilitate discussion. The SEF Team Emotional Assessment provides a list of emotions (table 1.1, page 16). Ask teammates to evaluate the degree to which these emotional states are present. The presence of each emotion is indicated by a number from 0–5, with 5 representing the greatest and 0 representing no presence of this emotional state. If a group is incredibly angry almost every day, a person might give the group a 5 for anger. If patience is rarely experienced, a person would rate that emotion with a 1 or even a 0.

If you are applying SEF to an entire staff, you will want to qualify this assessment by making sure people respond with what is truly common most of the time. If you ask a team about common emotional states before the holidays, for example, after the failure of a referendum, or just before summer vacation, it's likely that these variables might cloud their judgment. However, getting them to truly evaluate what's common most of the time can usually be accomplished with some reinforcement of that intent. This assessment should be taken individually and then discussed either in small groups or with the entire staff.

If you are applying strategic emotional focus to a smaller group, such as a department or school improvement committee, ask the group to limit its evaluation to the work of the group itself. In some cases, a department or subgroup may have a significantly different emotional tenor than the rest of the school.

Keep in mind that this evaluation is designed to gauge the strength of a full range of emotions. Of course, schools don't generally experience emotions like euphoria or modesty. However, the use of this instrument has helped many schools to become aware of exactly what they're feeling collectively and to be more thoughtful about what those feelings mean to their progress in learning.

Although schools may rarely discuss their levels of contentment, desire, alarm, or apprehension, these distinctly different emotions typically signal embedded issues that need to be resolved.

After using this assessment in a variety of locations in schools all over the world, I have found that there is always general agreement on which emotions dominate the local landscape. Asking each participant to total his or her scores from the negative and positive columns gives us a brief but powerful glimpse into the "typical" emotional mindset of the team. Interestingly, I have never given this instrument to a group in which there wasn't also agreement on which column of emotions, positive or negative, was predominant.

Table 1.1: SEF Team Assessment

Using a scale from 0, the lowest, to 5, the highest, rank the degree to which your organization or group experiences these emotions at work.

Positive Emotion	Score	Negative Emotion	Score
Acceptance		Agitation	
Amusement		Alarm	
Anticipation		Anger	
Awe		Angst	
Calmness		Apprehension	
Comfort		Bitterness	
Confidence		Boredom	
Contentment		Depression	
Courage		Disappointment	
Delight		Discontent	
Desire		Disgust	
Elation		Embarrassment	
Euphoria		Envy	
Gladness		Fear	
Glee		Frustration	
Gratitude		Grief	
Happiness		Guilt	
Honor		Hate	
Hope		Jealousy	
Humility		Loneliness	
Joy		Nervousness	
Kindness		Rage	
Love		Remorse	
Modesty		Self-pity	
Patience		Shame	
Peace		Shock	
Pride		Sorrow	
Surprise		Terror	
Suspense		Vulnerability	

Visit **go.solution-tree.com/leadership** to download and print this resource.

At this point, the team should resist any tendency to judge or analyze the answers or to identify the origin of the emotions that emerge.

Step Two: Reappraising the Emotional Response

In the field of psychology, the term *reappraisal* refers to our ability to conceptualize our emotions, consider their meaning, and reframe them before we act (Butler et al., 2003). Even though we want to be responsive to our emotional impulses, we have the capacity to reshape or reappraise our feelings (Butler et al., 2003: Gross, 1998, 2002; Gross & John, 2002). For example, we may be irritated by a colleague who interrupts us when we're trying to concentrate on grading a paper, but after reappraising the interaction, we recognize that our colleague's need to express himself was driven by something worth paying attention to. The frustration turns into a more empowering feeling of curiosity. The questions in table 1.2, based on our core knowledge about emotion, will help you reappraise your organization's emotional tendencies in light of how well they support the school's goals and mission.

Table 1.2: Reappraisal Questions

Answer the questions below using a scale from 0, the lowest, to 5, the highest.

1. How consistently do we seek out and support positive emotions?	
2. To what extent do we experience sagging emotions?	
3. How emotionally resilient are we?	
4. How much do we mute or deny any emotions?	
5. To what degree are we emotionally abundant?	
6. How wide a variety of emotions do we experience?	
7. To what extent do we ruminate or exaggerate our emotions?	
8. To what degree do we apply emotional energy and focus to issues that are relevant to our work?	
9. How aware are we of what our emotions are signaling about our work and about us?	
10. How often do we take the right actions in response to these emotions?	

Visit **go.solution-tree.com/leadership** to download and print this resource.

Step Three: Identifying the Desired Emotional Focus

Steps one and two of strategic emotional focus will inspire interesting, revealing, and collegial conversations. These conversations will likely identify challenges that need to be addressed and habits in the school that should change. Keep in mind that our individual and collective emotional states are a moving target. Emotions never completely sit still for us to manage and measure. Furthermore, our goal isn't to "reprogram" our emotions. Instead, the goal of this process is to become more acutely aware of the emotional states that are present and to take actions that will promote more empowering ones—ones that lead to deeper learning and greater levels of creativity. In this step, we will identify the emotions that are required to move the organization toward its goals, beginning with an emotional survey. Following are some sample survey questions and typical responses:

- **"What emotions do we express too often that don't serve our overall progress?"**

   Sample answers: anger, loneliness, self-pity

   You may have a very good reason to be angry, and it's important to be thoughtful about the cause of the signal and the actions you take, but spending an inordinate amount of time expressing anger won't serve your organizational goals.

- **"What emotions should we share and express more often that would serve us well?"**

   Sample answers: curiosity, courage, pride

   One school got to this step in the process and realized that despite the happiness, caring, and concern they shared for one another, they lacked two very important emotions—curiosity and courage. Although their school was relatively average, they decided they weren't average educators and could, in the end, do much more—and that curiosity and courage would be required.

- **"What goals do we have, and what emotions need to emerge to meet them?"**

Sample answers: Improve the average reading score in the school by 1.5 grade levels. Reduce the dropout rate from 25 percent to 10 percent in three years.

A school that wants to dramatically improve the low reading scores in second grade or reduce the high school dropout rate will need to be clear about the prominent emotions that need to emerge to bring that change to fruition. Goals may already exist in a strategic plan or school improvement outcome, but the goals identified here should be ones that are important to the people going through the exercise. A district goal, for example, of reducing redundant bus routes may do little to stir the emotions of a team of elementary teachers.

Step Four: Establishing Strategic Action

Actions create an opportunity to promote a particular emotional tenor. Going to a party or a funeral will likely dictate the emotions we experience during those events. Courage might be elicited by having to respond to a challenge. This step is not about identifying how we feel; it is about identifying the actions that are likely to lead us toward empowering emotions and the results they can bring.

Suppose, after taking the emotional survey, the group agrees that anger, loneliness, and self-pity are the prominent disempowering emotions in their school. After evaluating the origins of these states, the group could identify actions that would create an environment in which they were less likely to emerge. For example, loneliness can often be addressed with more collaboration. Self-pity might be reduced by canceling the Friday afternoon whining session. A school that is constantly angry may need to reflect and discuss the challenges at hand. Be specific about the actions that could be taken in response to the disempowering emotions.

Asking better questions, and asking them more often, could arouse curiosity. "What are other schools doing about this problem?" and "How can we fix that?" are two good questions. If several teachers tried a reading intervention with the goal of getting the school's most challenged readers up to state standard by the end of the year, courage might be awakened, and making that reading goal public could awaken the school's pride.

Suppose a school decides that meeting its goal of dramatically reducing the dropout rate requires patience, kindness, confidence, and a strong desire to succeed. The team would then need to examine the steps they can take to ensure the consistent presence of these emotions—perhaps beginning with several easily accomplished short-term goals that could generate the momentum needed to begin taking on more significant challenges.

Step Five: Reflecting, Committing, Measuring, and Starting Again

In step five of strategic emotional focus, teams make a commitment to reflect continually on this process. Examples of how this could be done include the following:

- **SEF-embedded meeting agendas**—If a team meets regularly, it should build in a feedback loop regarding SEF. If a series of plans has been established to promote courage or gratitude, review the implementation of those plans to see if progress is being made.

- **SEF-embedded school improvement process**—Embedding SEF strategies into the school improvement process makes a great deal of sense. If the plan is revised continuously throughout the year, why not also examine the source of the plan's power—emotion.

- **SEF subcommittees**—A school may consider asking a team of staff members to come together to form a subcommittee around this outcome. They could report on progress and ensure that the plans were actually implemented.

- **SEF blog or learning team**—By starting a local blog in which they reflect on the plans related to strategic emotional focus, the staff or a team could become much more reflective about the power of emotion in schools.

To make this process work, it is very important that a thoughtful learning leader create a habit of setting aside specific times for dealing with the power of emotions. If you don't take this time to strategically commit to reflection, it's likely that the notion of strategic emotional focus will quickly get put aside. This is because we tend to forget the power of emotion. In the day-to-day grind, it's easier to get caught up in the hypnosis of answering emails and going to meetings and to put aside the creative work that leads toward new outcomes and mental models.

Another way to ensure commitment and reflection is through measurement. By giving the emotional survey again later in the year, having another thoughtful discussion, and then comparing the results, it is likely that team members will either see some growth or know why they did not.

The pursuit of positive emotional power never ends. Since people come and go in an organization and our emotions continue to shape and reshape who we are and how we interact with the world, it's likely that you'll always be restarting this process. However, with time spent using the tool of strategic emotional focus, team members will become much more adroit at understanding the power of emotion and will very quickly learn to react on their feet to identify opportunities to grow and evolve.

By supporting a culture empowered by positive emotions, learning leaders can become experts at bringing out the greatness in others.

CHAPTER 2

Acknowledging and Reframing Fear

As we saw in the previous chapter, emotion is the lynchpin for learning. We now focus on the one emotional state that halts organizational learning in its tracks—fear (Wood, Norris, Waters, & Stoldt, 2008; Sprinkle, Hunt, Simonds, & Comandena, 2006; Lipton, 2008).

From an evolutionary standpoint, emotions operate in direct proportion to our needs. Curiosity, for example, keeps us innovative and allows us to improve our living conditions. Love keeps us from spending too much time at work and ensures that we take the time to pass on our genes. Empathy and sorrow add to the complexity of our human experience and connect us to one another. Arguably, however, our successful evolution as a species has had a lot more to do with our sensitivity to fear than to any other emotional state. Fear kept your ancestors away from bears and keeps you from using your cell phone while driving. Fear gets you to temporarily suspend emotional states like love, empathy, and sorrow when your survival is on the line. Our fear sensitivity is always there waiting to interrupt the broadcast.

Fear, then, is a very good thing. If you are following a leader who claims to be fearless, you might want to give him a two- or three-step head start. However, while fear is great for promoting survival, it's a terrible emotional state to be in when trying to engage in deep learning (Oathes & Ray, 2008; Shu-Shen, 2008).

School leaders have an interesting relationship with fear. Some of us have used it as a tool to govern and control; others have tried to deny its existence or ignored its powerful psychological influence. The current emphasis on accountability, which demands both quality and measurable levels of heterogeneous equity—outcomes that arguably have never been achieved before at any international level in pre-K–12 education, generates a great deal of fear.

The more school leaders can deal with and transform fear in schools, the more successfully they will be able to lead deep and meaningful change.

Core Knowledge: Fear

Physiologically speaking, fear activates our neural circuits, resulting in behaviors directed toward survival (Osinsky et al., 2008; Sebrant, 2008; Yap & Richardson, 2007). Fear puts us into action and gets us to prepare our defense against an outside threat (Blanchard, Griebel, & Blanchard, 2001). Unfortunately, while fear is a real issue in many schools, it is also needlessly activated at times when survival is not an issue and the threats are imaginary ones. This section looks at our core knowledge of fear in regard to school leadership.

Survival Is More Important Than School

Survival is our brain's one-word mission statement: every aspect of our physical and emotional makeup is designed to promote it (Mac-Donald, 2008; Lipton, 2008; Bateson et al., 2004). That is why fear, once we are introduced to it, has the potential to completely distract us from everything else. The brain has an unbreakable habit of putting increased attention on threatening stimuli before recognizing or responding to anything nonthreatening (Garner, Mogg, & Bradley, 2006; Lees, Mogg, & Bradley, 2005). Neuroscientists have labeled this inner mechanism *predatory imminence*. Fundamentally, predatory imminence works like a thermometer: as threats around us increase, our sense of predatory imminence rises and assigns them a relative threat rating (Fanselow & Lester, 1988). A large dog off a leash in the distance may distract you, stimulating a warning level of predatory imminence. If that dog starts moving in your direction, you get nervous, and your sense of predatory imminence registers an increased threat level. If the dog then growls and moves aggressively toward you, your sense of predatory imminence will sound the alarm, demanding that your senses take notice and that you prepare to defend yourself.

Clearly, the degree to which this most basic aspect of our learning system is engaged determines how much of our attention is pulled away from our work (Fanselow & Lester, 1988). We have always had a sense that leaders need to approach change carefully and build trust first. Now we know why.

Fight or Flight—Is Your School Doing Too Much of Both?

Fight or flight is the term that neuroscientists assign to the physical response that occurs during stress or fear. While predatory imminence evaluates the potential threats around us, fight or flight is a separate internal mechanism designed to respond to the fear or threat. In fight-or-flight mode, our heart rate increases, our blood pressure goes up, our senses become more alert, our muscles tense, our palms get sweaty, the blood-clotting factors in our bloodstream increase, and all of our physical centers related to movement and action become mobilized (Machado, Kazama, & Bachevalier, 2009; Romero & Butler, 2007; Lipton, 2008).

Fight or flight physically prepares the body to deal with fear the same way a faucet regulates the flow of water: a minor threat may make us jittery; a major one will kick our bodies into a wide-open response. This measured response to fear makes a great deal of sense. Imagine how tired you would feel if every threat you perceived was met with an all-out, heart-pounding, physiological response?

However, there are two major problems with fight or flight as it relates to our work in schools. First, even though you are physically at your best when you are ready for a fight, you are mentally at your worst. Your senses may be alert, but your brain is thinking about survival. These reactions are governed by the amygdalae, a pair of small structures deep within the brain that retain vivid emotional memories. If you were hit and nearly killed as a child by a fire engine, your amygdalae might throw you uncontrollably into fight or flight at the sound of a siren, or just the sight of red flashing lights. So while your cerebral cortex (or gray matter) is good with details, the amygdalae keep a less specific, blunt record of your deepest emotional memories. This is why, when we are angry, we sometimes cannot think of what to say. The amygdalae know how to tell us to fight or run, but we need our cerebral cortex to come up with pithy one-liners in the face of a public critic.

The second major problem with fight or flight is that this highly inefficient mechanism cannot distinguish animal fear from psychological fear (Wolfe, 2001). This means that it can cause the pit to form in your stomach, the sweat to break out on your back, and the palpitations to begin in your heart just as easily before you give a speech as it can when you're walking through a dangerous jungle. When you're afraid, you're afraid. Most neuroscientists agree that this system was not designed to be stimulated as often as it is in so-called civilized life and that its overstimulation leads to a number of negative physical and mental consequences (Machado, Kazama, & Bachevalier, 2009; Romero & Butler, 2007). Every time your body gets ready for a nonexistent fight, it needs to later release energy to bring it back to a state of relaxation—which is why we often need to walk off stress (Halm, 2009). This is important information for learning leaders, because so many things we do in school can trigger psychological or even physical fear.

Several years ago, while leading some after-school training with a large staff of teachers, I noticed several factors that were probably triggering some degree of fight or flight, including these:

- Metal-back chairs—The teachers were sitting in stiff, metal-back chairs. Most likely, while they were working with me, their brains were quietly monitoring their physical discomfort, alert to whether it was getting more intense. We may consciously know that we are not in physical danger, but our survival mechanisms and sense of predatory imminence are suspicious and remain attentive to further discomfort even as we try to keep our attention elsewhere.

- Fatigue—These teachers were tired. Being asked to work hard when we are tired brings on stress, because there is a little voice inside that always wants to save energy in case we need to fight or flee to survive. We can physically push through fatigue quite effectively; our bodies just want a good reason to do so.

- Fluorescent lights and television—The fluorescent lights hummed loudly overhead while wall-mounted TVs flickered silently. Both of these devices caused neurological distraction

(Soo-Young & Jong-Jin, 2006; Christakis, Zimmerman, DiGiuseppe., & McCarty, 2004). Our eyes can become transfixed when watching television or when we are in fluorescent lighting due to the stimulation created in the brain, and flickering light has been shown to trigger fear (Baumgartner, Valko, Esslen, & Jancke, 2006; Anderson, 2007). That is why it is used in advertising. Fear gets and keeps our attention—and sometimes we are afraid to look away.

- Feelings of powerlessness—The staff didn't know I was coming, and they didn't have any say in the content of their training. My presence didn't give them a direct sense of panic. However, the uncertainty of the situation probably triggered a quiet sense of powerlessness that left them wondering, "What else am I going to experience while working at this school that will be beyond my control?"

- Teacher bullies—Several teacher bullies had been publicly humiliating victims of their choice for over a decade. When I sought participation from the group, I saw fear in the eyes of several newer teachers anticipating the launch of sarcastic verbal bombs from these angry colleagues, who were waiting on the sidelines to attack.

Any steps we take to make the learning environment psychologically safer will result in greater focus and learning potential. Chapter 8 will address some of the fundamentals of creating an ideal learning environment.

Fear Is Something We Love to Share

Emotional congruence is a relatively new term in the study of emotions. Scientists have discovered that people in groups tend to align their emotions (Stout, 2007). If we walk into a room full of people who are laughing, we usually start laughing, too. From an evolutionary standpoint, this ability has helped us pull together when times were tough. However, we need to keep in mind that, because we're always ready to share our emotional state and fear is such a powerful emotion, sharing fear also comes naturally to us.

We also know that some people are more acutely aware than others of potential threats. In particular, nervous or anxious individuals devote a great deal more of their cognitive attention to scanning their surroundings for potentially threatening stimuli or threatening information (Fox, Russo, Bowles, & Dutton, 2001). In less scientific terms, this means there are people in your organization who subconsciously worry quite a bit more than others about survival. This causes them to react more emotionally in certain situations or retreat to negative behaviors at the first sign of a threat. Because emotional congruence is such a powerful factor in our lives, the fear that is being fervently shared may create a much more pronounced focus on this emotion in your school than you realize.

Fearing Change Is Natural

Being fearless is a myth, because we rely on fear for survival and can never turn off that tendency (Mogg & Bradley, 1998; Verduyn, Delvaux, Van Coillie, Tuerlinckx, & Van Mechelen, I.; 2009; Van den Berg & ter Heijne, 2005). Courageous actions may help convince our system of predatory imminence that we are strong and resilient, but we will continue to be aware of and monitor the world around us for perceived threats. Even many seasoned performers feel fear before taking the stage, but their experience and preparation keep it from taking over.

Assuming we can approach change in school without fear ignores a basic principle of what it means to be human (Mathews & MacLeod, 1994; Mineka & Ohman, 2002). At some level, our jobs may bore or frustrate us, but they also provide safety and psychological equilibrium, and a regular paycheck provides security, now and in the future. Even if leaders are not satisfied with their work, having their basic needs met helps keep fear at bay. By introducing change that challenges behavior patterns in school, we are in essence putting that safety at risk. Will a new change at school suddenly push our capacities to the point where we can't keep up? Will our inability to manage change make us useless to the herd? Our logical mind reminds us that we can adapt to change when it comes along, but our deep wish to be safe is an animal instinct that we have to overcome every time we attempt to make a major alteration in our lives. Leaders need to be aware that, at a deep psychological level, fearing change is natural and that supporting people in overcoming even low levels of nervousness will pay good dividends in the long term.

Teaming Foils Fear, Isolation Fuels It

In schools that don't have highly functioning formal teams, powerful informal groups may evolve organically based on social interaction. These teams are held together by history and a genuine mutual care and concern for one another. In times of celebration or trouble, these groups quickly find one another and team up to provide direction and support. There is safety in numbers.

Some schools do an outstanding job of creating such deeply interconnected groups. Throughout these schools, teams and groups of teachers and staff abound who are confident and willing to take risks in the name of growth and change. When problems arise, they respond to them.

At less-effective schools, people are often completely incapable of coming together to reach a desired goal. Often, this inability is driven by old patterns of isolation. When staff members are not part of a team, it's easy for them to feel alone, and that can breed fear. We explore this issue further in chapter 9 in the context of collaboration.

Using Fear as a Stick Shuts Down Learning

Fear of drowning keeps you out of the ocean when there is a riptide, fear of its owner keeps the family cat off the kitchen table, and fear of the whip drove slaves to build the pyramids. Leaders have historically used the power of fear in more subtle ways as well. For example, organizational leadership has a theory called *management by exception*, according to which leaders confront any behavior deemed inconsistent with the work standard (Liu, Shih, & Kao, 2001). Under this management style, punishing failure to follow the rule is considered more effective than encouraging the rule's acceptance. The goal of the work becomes the avoidance of the boss' wrath.

Leaders who are not terribly creative often use fear simply because they can't elicit followership any other way. Inspiring others to be thoughtful and creative takes skill and focus. Inspiring through fear takes a big stick—and sticks are a lot easier to find. But as we have seen, any team that is motivated by fear will not be functioning at its best, because part of the brain of each of its members is diverting mental energy toward survival.

In addition, when leaders use fear to control others they have to be willing to constantly raise the stakes. Psychologists refer to this as *habituation*. In basic terms, habituation means that individuals or teams can get used to almost anything if they endure it long enough. Technically, habituation is a form of learning in which the repetition of a certain stimulus ultimately lessens the intensity of the response (Stout, 2007). If a school uses fear as a means of control, habituation creates the need to continually raise the stakes to get the same result. This leads to an escalation in behaviors like aggression, anger, and contempt—all of which are promulgated by fear.

From a learning leadership standpoint, we can see the advantages of working with a leader whose honesty makes us feel safe. An honest leader isn't going to surprise us with unpleasant threats; and we will always know what to expect from him or her. Perhaps this is why honesty is widely regarded as perhaps the most essential leadership attribute (Kouzes & Posner, 2009).

Fear May Be Masked

Our natural instinct in schools is to deny our fear in order not to appear weak or cowardly. Perhaps this goes back to our earliest roots, when the strong prevailed and the weak were sorted out. Feeling fear, however, may in fact be a sign of wisdom, sensitivity, and overall readiness.

Nevertheless, we have learned to use other emotions to mask our fear. Deep down, some of the most negative, angry, jealous, and frustrated school staff are well-intentioned educators who are actually filled with fear and uncertainty but use these other feelings to mask it. At one point in their careers, they may have taken chances and failed, and rather than muster up the strength to overcome failure, they became unwilling to take risks again. Wounded, woozy, and seeking shelter, these individuals use negativity, anger, and lashing out as a shield both to protect themselves from experiences that might bring more fear and to keep us from seeing the fear that already exists within them.

This doesn't mean that angry, negative staff members will suddenly see the light once you assure them they are safe or that you understand their plight. Some staff may never unpack or resolve their masking patterns. However, deep down, most educators want to make a significant contribution. Rather than reacting to a mask of jealousy or anger, a learning leader can make things better for everyone by working to address the uncertainty lurking below the surface—or at least by being mindful of the dynamic of masking when dealing with difficult faculty members. Awareness of this pattern can keep learning leaders from being pulled, through emotional congruence, into negative emotional states like fear.

Context Affects Fear

Because the brain is always scanning the environment for potential threats, context can contribute to and amplify the emotion of fear (Larsen, 2000; Tice & Bratslavsky, 2000). For example, some schools have extremely antiquated areas for teachers to work together in—rooms that are dark or small, stifling, and uncomfortable. Faced with meeting in a space like this, an extremely fear-sensitive individual may feel a great deal of anxiety. A conference room in which a difficult or embarrassing meeting was once held may evoke feelings of anxiety in participants who use it on subsequent occasions.

While leaders can't always know or understand the exact ways that context stimulates fear, it is nevertheless important to keep context in mind when trying to stimulate deep organizational learning. In order to ensure that context won't become an obstacle, many leaders find that holding a retreat away from the work environment is helpful. When we get away from the workplace, we see our work and ourselves with new eyes.

Catastrophizing Keeps Us Fearful

Another habit related to fear involves *catastrophizing,* a term used to describe the persistent focus on worst-case scenarios (Hunt, Milonova, & Moshier, 2009; Moldovan, Onac, Vantu, Szentagotai, & Onac, 2009; Sullivan, Lynch, Clark, Mankovsky, & Sawynok, 2008). Given our natural desire to avoid what we fear, it may seem counterintuitive to focus so intently on all the bad things that might happen. Looked at from a survival perspective, however, it makes perfect sense. If an early human had a bad experience with a mountain lion and lived to tell about it, the word spread with great intensity. As with most of our natural learning systems, these emotional impulses served us well, but because the brain can't distinguish psychological from animal fear, and because most of our struggles in school are not life or death, amping up the message isn't always productive. As a result, learning leaders must work to reduce catastrophizing behaviors.

Since catastrophizing is often done in pockets throughout the organization, learning leaders should actively work together to extinguish the fires of anticipated calamity and focus instead on solutions.

Reflect, Consolidate, Act, Laugh

Reflection and *consolidation* refer to the processes by which the brain takes time to integrate our experiences in relationship to our background, values, and belief systems. When we do this, we're typically much more thoughtful in our actions. Refection and consolidation keep fear in perspective.

Strategic *action* is another powerful antidote to fear. As schools become more adroit at working together and overcoming challenges, they also become more confident and powerful. More confident schools may feel the influence of fear, but they learn to act thoughtfully rather than react quickly when dealing with it.

Finally, *humor* helps defuse stress and distract us from fear (Kangasharju & Nikko, 2009). Organizational research has shown that humor helps to release repressed emotions, tensions, and stress and has also been shown to enhance team members' self-esteem, manage embarrassment, and improve group solidarity (Dziegielewski, Jacinto, Laudaio, & Legg-Rodriguez, 2003; Kangasharju & Nikko, 2009). Successful schools know how to laugh in the face of difficult challenges. Although change is serious business that requires work, energy, and focus, laughter along the way breaks tension and allows us to relax—and relaxation is a great gift to the brain.

Solutions in Action: Change, Analysis, and Reframing

This section presents the change, analysis, and reframing strategy for directly and systematically confronting fear in schools and removing some of the hindrances it brings to learning. This strategy is effective because it allows fearful individuals to express themselves without getting stuck in a particular emotion. The strategy (fig. 2.1) is simple, but it must be implemented systematically. Teams that use it consistently will get better at it and learn to move more quickly from level to level when facing change.

The change, analysis, and reframing strategy is intuitive, and some teams follow it quite naturally. However, by using it in a disciplined and purposeful way, participants are much more likely to be reflective, keep fear in perspective, and improve their individual and collective capacity to generate new solutions. The strategy can be used either when confronting significant change, like the adoption of a new schedule or a major reform to instruction and assessment, or more extemporaneously when small groups or teams are faced with change. The model can be expanded or simplified depending on the variables being analyzed. However, it is important to follow the four steps of the model in order.

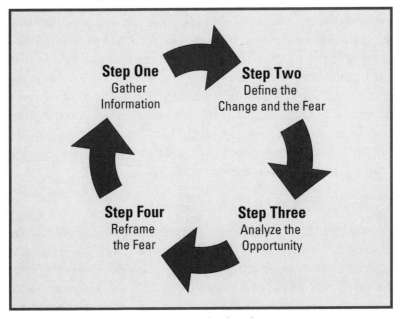

Step One
Gather
Information

Step Two
Define the
Change and the Fear

Step Four
Reframe
the Fear

Step Three
Analyze the
Opportunity

Figure 2.1: The change, analysis, and reframing strategy.

Step One: Gather Information

When facing a change that has the potential to create fear, it is important to gather as much information as possible regarding the change as a means of preparing the group for the process. Again, depending on the complexity of the change, this might involve inviting to the meeting key people in the organization who are either responsible for certain decisions or aware of details that might be related to them. If the change, such as a new set of graduation requirements or a dramatic cut in the district budget, came from outside the school, it is helpful to gather as much information as possible from those external sources before moving forward.

Step Two: Define the Change and the Fear

Next, it is essential to directly and collaboratively identify all the issues associated with this change that may arouse fear. These can be identified by answering the following questions.

What Does the Change Really Mean?

When change is upon us, we often start reacting before we have evaluated the real significance of the change. One group may immediately interpret a budget cut from the state and a lack of new materials to mean simply that they can't implement the new math curriculum. Other groups may decide after reflection that it requires a recalibration of their efforts to raise money and develop the local curriculum. Being thoughtful about what a change means frames the work from the outset and shapes our efforts going forward. Ideally, teams or groups look at a number of possible meanings related to the new information and then collaborate on a common one.

What's the Worst That Could Happen?

The next step is to discuss the fears aloud, no matter how rational or irrational they are. As we have noted, that fear may also show up in the form of stress, anger, and even confusion. The group's goal should be to come up with an inclusive list of all potential fears. Don't worry about exaggeration—it's better at this point to ask questions and get all the fears out than to keep them hidden away.

Suppose teachers authoring end-of-course assessments fear that they can't meet expectations or that their contributions to the assessment won't be seen as valuable. They may worry that they are losing control of their classrooms by giving up the power to control grades and instruction. Common assessments offer great opportunities, but teachers would be kidding themselves if they weren't anxious about these issues. The more team members openly discuss their anxieties, the more skillful they become at being honest during this phase.

This step is also an opportunity for the naysayers to have their say and the worrywarts to openly worry, although it is essential for the group to place limits on the time it spends dealing with these concerns. The more intense or personal the change, the more time the group will need to process it. Just as in brainstorming we accept all ideas, here it is important not to dismiss any fears as irrelevant or too extreme. This step also requires some trial and error. Groups that move on from it too quickly may later realize they have not exorcised all the fears. Or—and this is the more common pattern—the fearmongers in the group may prefer to remain at this stage and will resist moving on.

At this point, the team should not try to come up with answers to the fears being presented. That challenge comes later in the process.

What's the Best That Could Happen?

The previous question allowed the worriers to worry. This question allows the dreamers to dream, and hopefully everyone—including the worriers—will articulate big dreams. At this level, the team should wonder aloud what would happen if they were outrageously successful. Could a team, for example, experience a budget cut and imagine itself growing at previously unmatched levels? Could common assessment bring the staff together and dramatically improve instruction? The endpoint for this aspect of the process should include a list of great outcomes. Again, the list shouldn't be edited or tampered with at this point.

Most schools hesitate to dream because they are constantly brought back down to earth by their fears. When one teacher exclaims, "What if our test scores got better?!" a colleague responds with, "But what if we run out of money?!" Depending on the circumstances, both might be right. However, it's tough to solve problems if we construct the best- and worst-case scenarios simultaneously. The change, analysis, and reframing strategy breaks up these phases, requiring participants to first focus on the possibilities for success and then acknowledge the potential for fear and frustration. In brainstorming the best that could happen, it's important that team members not get bogged down with analyzing actual challenges related to implementation. Due to scale, costs, and so on, not every great idea is actionable. However, participants should feel free to identify the best-case scenarios without constraint.

Step Three: Analyze the Opportunity

Now that the team has gathered all the necessary information to begin this brainstorming process and has come up with a list of reactions from the dreamers, the fearmongers, and everyone in between, they are ready to move forward to the analysis.

The team should begin by more carefully considering the list of possibilities generated from their "What's the best that could happen?" discussion. It's important to start here, because as teams grow in their capacity to collaborate, this step often yields remarkably innovative and important solutions, which the team may be excited about pursuing. The list of ideas or suggestions that was generated may, in fact, negate or make moot many of the concerns brought up by the fearmongers. Within the analysis phase, the team may also identify some solutions as well intentioned but not useful at this time. Other ideas when pursued in more detail may emerge as actionable steps that could bring levels of value to the organization that hadn't been anticipated. The team should not feel it must articulate strategic plans around actionable suggestions brought up at this point in the process. This session should end with a list of potentially helpful ideas that may require further analysis and planning.

Step Four: Reframe the Fear

Despite the best intentions, a number of issues related to change may continue to make team members fearful, even in the face of potentially exciting innovations. It is important from an emotional standpoint to be honest about these fears and to address them directly. At this stage, evaluate whether any of the "What's the worst that could happen?" scenarios represent an emotional signal we should actually pay attention to. For example, the stress and fear a team feels about a change that could have a negative impact on work they've done over a ten-year period to improve the curriculum might actually be well founded.

The reframing process requires participants to examine potential negative consequences, reframe the challenge away from fear, potentially introduce a new emotional mindset, and proactively take steps to investigate their concerns. For example, teachers who are concerned that somehow change will demean their efforts might decide to put some of that energy into curiosity. They may choose to join a larger group and proactively investigate other schools that have attempted this change in order to determine if their concerns are warranted. Getting curious, taking action, and doing research is a way of formally reframing the fear in an empowering, thoughtful way that can ultimately result in either putting the fears to bed or informing the team of a potential pitfall that our fear sensors were wise enough to identify.

By taking the steps to thoughtfully and formally reframe the fear, we bring new emotion and action to the table, prepare to respond in a direct and focused manner, and diminish fear's capacity to simply nip away at us. At the end of the reframing session, the group should leave empowered with the notion that a plan is in place to address its concerns regarding change.

In this chapter, we have learned about the power of fear, some of the neurological reasons it exists, and the steps we can take to minimize the development of a culture of fear in schools. Although fear will always be with us, we have the power to decide on the degree to which we are going to allow it to influence our work. By thoughtfully reframing fear with the change, analysis, and reframing strategy, we're much more likely to respond appropriately to this basic impulse whenever we feel it without missing the message it's sending.

Learning leaders who know how fear works are much more likely to make the best choices in working with their staff and to prevent learning from being derailed by this emotional state. We can go beyond fear to where most teams never go—to that sweet spot in the change process where groups are brave enough to dream big.

CHAPTER 3

The Impact of Stress on Organizational Learning

Judy was a forty-three-year-old single mother and assistant principal in a very large high school, as well as a doctoral student. She would come into the teachers' lounge like a prizefighter between rounds, huffing and puffing. Her teacher friends hovered around her, providing both coaching and solace, knowing the bell would soon ring and the fight would start all over again. Judy would always have an avalanche of new problems to share with her friends. She practically lived at the office, never ate breakfast, grabbed lunch and dinner from a vending machine, smoked when she could, and died on the job before spring break.

Stress can take good people like Judy away from us long before their time. In addition to the potential physical dangers of stress, we are beginning to understand how it diminishes our individual and collective capacity to learn. Being under stress undermines a group's ability to make decisions and follow predetermined choices, and it creates the desire to gravitate toward what's immediately comforting, convenient, or easy (Tice, Bratslavsky, & Baumeister, 2001; Vohs et al., 2008). This pattern doesn't often result in goal attainment and can lead to the emergence of more problems (Baas, DeDreu, & Nijstad, 2008).

In schools today, expectations of performance continue to rise, the complexity of the work is increasing, and by affording teachers and principals greater autonomy, we've undoubtedly created new expectations—all of which certainly contribute to increased stress. Stress can cause a great deal of distraction, and when a school begins to experience high levels of stress on a consistent basis, its individual and collective brainpower begins to be systematically siphoned off, reducing the capacity to innovate and evolve. By establishing a process to address stress directly, learning leaders can reduce one of the most powerful hindrances to organizational learning and create a culture that will be healthier for everyone involved.

Core Knowledge: Stress

The key statements about stress that follow will help learning leaders better understand why stress occurs, when it occurs, and how it is unwittingly nurtured and sustained.

We Don't Work Better Under Stress

Many teams believe they work much better when they are under stress. Is this true? Sometimes yes, but mostly no. When we sense something that makes us feel stress, the brain releases hormones that temporarily change our physiology. Small amounts of stress may actually ignite our consciousness and help us focus on learning. Large amounts of stress, however, have a negative impact on the brain and can impede the learning process (Sapolsky, 1998; Gadzella, Masten, & Zascavage, 2009).

For example, a public commitment to creating a new assessment for the school improvement plan might generate accelerated expectations, which may create a level of stress just high enough to inspire the group to work harder, pull together, support one another, and in the end, become much more focused. A public commitment may also trigger emotions like pride and courage—feelings that inspire energy, focus, action, and attention—and help us ignore what may be only petty differences. More commonly, however, schools find themselves under the kind of stress that is not helpful and that usually arises for the wrong reasons, like procrastination, unclear or unrealistic expectations, or an exaggerated response to some challenge or goal. These stressors interrupt learning and lead to distraction, frustration, and fatigue. Teams in schools that have a larger purpose or focus don't need the momentary thrill of almost missing a deadline to take meaningful action or to become inspired. These less distracted and more focused teams conjure up emotional energy and focus due to their vision of where they are going.

Teams that claim to work better under stress may be underestimating themselves: the stress may motivate them, but *less* stress with more focus would take them much further.

Stress Is in Your Head

A woman screaming in a dark hallway or shadowy figures looming in the distance might make you laugh if you're in a funhouse. Under other conditions, those sights and sounds will produce a great deal of stress. The context makes all the difference.

School leaders can't pretend they're at the funhouse when stress is on the rise, but the best leaders have a way of maintaining an even, positive emotional tone despite what's going on around them. When others try to make the conversation about the tensions that exist, these leaders take the opportunity to inject strategy, optimism, and hope. When others infuse a situation with fear and stress, these leaders inspire, focus, and encourage the pursuit of creative solutions. Like fear, stress is an important signal. When we feel it, we should not simply ignore it; however, the actions we take upon recognizing the stress signal will define our success as a learning organization. The decision whether to indulge an emotional impulse or reframe and make thoughtful use of it represents the fork in the road that learning leaders must face.

Stress Increases When It's Shared

In social situations, stress is very quickly transmitted from one person to another, and sharing this emotion escalates its intensity (Ludick, Alexander, & Carmichael, 2007; McAllister, Thomas, Wilson, & Green, 2009). The more we share our stress, the more powerful it becomes.

Almost every school has *stress dealers*, who show up in two forms. The first type is hooked on stress and looking for company. He is often well intentioned, disorganized, and outwardly frustrated much of the time. Sitting next to him may make you feel a sense of his ongoing "dis-ease." Because he's so caught up in his own stress cycle, the stress dealer assumes everyone interacts with the world the way he does and is eager to share his state.

The second type of stress dealer uses stress to manipulate others. This group includes teachers who try to demean the efforts of a principal by associating his or her decisions with high levels of stress and warning colleagues of the mountain of work this will create. Staff members who use stress strategically may not be all that stressed themselves; however, they have come to recognize intuitively that it can be a powerful way to grab attention. Principals who are deliberate stress dealers may attempt to associate high levels of stress with a teacher request—deliberately exaggerating potential negative parental or student responses—in order to keep from taking action.

As with fear, our ability to share stress so effectively may be due to the survival experiences of our ancestors. However, most stress in schools, like most fear, is psychological, and the rapid ramping up of stress levels can detract from efforts to learn, grow, and improve (Compton, 2003; Pekrun, Maier, & Elliot, 2009). Drug dealers look for territory where the misery index is high and people lack hope and direction (Hutton, 2005). Stress dealers look for the same fertile soil, but as soon as the staff find focus, hope, and direction, the dealer loses most of his customers (Hirsch, Hayes, & Mathews, 2009).

Stress Levels Are Determined by Emotional Set Points

Our bodies naturally monitor a number of essential biological set points, such as body temperature and blood pressure, to sustain life. When we begin to feel even a subtle threat to these internal life-sustaining set points, we feel a stress response (Seidl, 2009). The response depends on both our experience and the context we find ourselves in. A room that is slowly losing its oxygen will produce universal feelings of discomfort and distraction, our body's way of telling us that something is amiss and that our attention is required. Less predictable is the way each of us responds to challenges to our psychological comfort or safety. Someone from Arizona attending a summer conference in Chicago, when it's 95 degrees, will have a different feeling about how hot it is than someone from Ohio.

Each school collectively establishes its own set points. School staff who have had success in managing emotions and working together will approach a new, rigorous challenge with the confidence that they can deal with it. At another school, people might find a less formidable challenge completely overwhelming and immediately begin to share high levels of stress with one another, crippling their progress and making work much less enjoyable. Learning leaders understand that these emotional set points don't change overnight. It takes time and deliberate effort to begin to adjust a set point so that less stress and more progress and learning emerge.

Adapting to Stress Isn't the Solution

When we learn to accept persistent stress in our lives, psychologists say we've made an *adaptation* (Hastings & Hastings, 2008). Prisoners of war who are held for years may never get comfortable with their conditions, but they find ways to survive. A school facing a budget crisis may decide that a needed change will take longer to implement and that in the meantime adapting to the stress is all they can do.

On the other hand, accommodating an overtly racist or sexist staff member could be tremendously harmful to a school and damage its capacity to ultimately come together, learn, and grow. Similarly, adaptation to the disappointment of underperformance can lead to continued low levels of achievement later. Adapting to small levels of stress may sometimes be prudent, but in most cases, dealing with stress directly is a better option for learning leaders (Lamontagne, Keegel, Louie, Ostry, & Landsbergis, 2007; Palmer & Puri, 2006).

Distraction Can Relieve or Exacerbate Stress

Since stress is so omnipresent and we are inherently predisposed to move away from it, it's not surprising that one of the strategies we use is distraction (Jacobs, 2003). Again, as with fear, a brief distraction gives the brain a respite and occasionally brings fresh energy to a problem. More often, however, schools seek distractions that are more complex and more destructive. Learning leaders recognize that a high number of distractions in a school may be a symptom of unresolved stress.

For example, a school might choose to distract itself from stressful news about low reading scores or high failure rates on state tests by planning the next party or dissecting the student dress code. The danger of distraction is threefold: time is wasted, issues go unresolved, and new problems are created.

Multitasking When Stressed Minimizes Brain Function

Groups that feel stressed will try to overwhelm themselves with activities in the mistaken belief that action alone will lead to progress. However, it may be an illusory progress. Brain imaging techniques tell us that, neurologically speaking, the brain exerts more effort writing an essay or reading a good book than in trying to do three or four less mentally taxing things at once. Surfing the Internet, watching TV, and talking on the phone all at once may give us the feeling of being busy. However, with each division of our attention, there is a net loss in our capacity to learn and focus (Wolfe, 2001; Dehaene, 2005; Kujala et al., 2007).

Schools that are doing too much at one time may be unknowingly distracting themselves from the deep and difficult thinking necessary to drive change. Learning leaders do not confuse multitasking with movement and progress.

Your Allostatic Load

Stress is not only a major distraction for schools trying to learn and grow together—it can also make us angry, exhausted, and unhealthy. The level of stress in our bodies is often referred to as an *allostatic load*. Lots of stress, or a heavy allostatic load, leads to cardiovascular disease, impaired immunity, obesity, and bone-demineralization (Rozanski, Blumenthal, & Kaplan, 1999; McEwen, 2004).

It is estimated that 70 percent of all U.S. healthcare visits are stress-related (Noyce, 2003). Stress-related absenteeism, company medical expenses, and decreased productivity cost U.S. employers in excess of one hundred eighty billion dollars each year (Darr & Johns, 2008; Angliss, 2008). Restless and stressed-out Americans spend six hundred and fifty million per year on sleeping pills; four million Americans abuse prescription drugs and are addicted to stimulants, tranquilizers, or painkillers (Smeltz, 2007; Petrecca, 2007). Prolonged stress can distract us from our purposes, increase mental fatigue, and deregulate hormonal activity, thus promoting depressive illness and the atrophy of nerve cells in the brain (Rozanski, Blumenthal, & Kaplan, 1999; McEwen & Lasley, 2003). In addition to its impact on health, this very prevalent response can have an insidious impact on organizational learning. Stress in a group can lead to feelings of helplessness; it can also sabotage brain functions, again reducing a group's collective learning power (Caine, Caine, McClintic, & Klimek, 2005).

Imagine the missed opportunities lost over decades of stress! Imagine how much more a school could get done if the staff could reduce stress and nurture the creative energies that are waiting to be released!

Patterns of Group Stress Response

Stress shared within a group can create reactions that may have long-term implications for its progress. Some psychologists believe that groups as large as an entire nation can share stress and may experience post-traumatic stress after a difficult national or international event (Stout, 2007). Let's consider some patterns of stress response in schools today.

The Angry and At-Wit's-End Group

This type of group can be angry and aggressive, both within the school and beyond. Some individuals come to school with personal anger already brewing, and the workplace is simply where they display it. Eventually, the team as a whole constantly demonstrates an angry, stressed, and at-wit's-end demeanor. These groups may rage against each other, the organization, or larger entities beyond the school.

Stress that's shared in a group is likely to create an intense, collective, fight-or-flight reaction (Bushman, Baumeister, & Phillips, 2001). As we learned in the previous chapter, this physiological response is quite effective when facing bears but ineffective when facing problems that require thoughtful, collaborative innovation. This type of group regards challenges or problems as personal affronts and prefers rattling sabers to learning and growth.

The Exhausted Group

Exhausted groups may express feelings of being at a tipping point, unable to take on one more challenge. Even minor adjustments to the rhythms or procedures of the school may be met with eyes rolled up in collective disbelief. Exhausted groups might also have once been angry and at their wit's end but found that if they act exhausted all the time, less is expected of them. All of us have waved the white flag at times, seeking temporary refuge from a storm. However, these groups rely heavily on this strategy, and they have lost their capacity to deal with stress by taking action to resolve a challenge.

The Manic, Last-Minute Group

Manic, last-minute groups are always rushing to beat the clock. They constantly feel a sense of panic, because as soon as they finish one last-minute deadline, they realize another is almost past. When they have lead time they squander it, since deadlines don't really mean much until they are looming and the stress begins to wash over them.

Procrastination is often seen as a shortcoming in commitment and a failure of time management. Individuals and groups who regularly do things at the last minute often achieve poor results, have higher levels of stress, and experience diminished levels of health and wellness (Gura, 2008).

Rushing to beat a deadline can make us feel needed, relevant, and even vital. Manic, last-minute groups are not, however, successful at leading deep, meaningful, and sustainable school improvement because they are far too frantic to take the time necessary to reflect on their work and think strategically about the next step.

The Looking-at-the-Pavement-While-Driving Group

Consider one's line of vision when driving a car on a cross-country trip. If you are cruising through the mountains at forty miles per hour and look off into the distance, the world seems to come at you rather slowly; you will notice the pleasant greenery arching into the air on beautiful blue-green hills. However, if you shift your gaze to stare down at the pavement just in front of the car, you have very little perspective on what is coming or where you have just been, and forty miles per hour seems like blinding speed. Groups in schools often do the same thing: they get caught up in the details of the moment whizzing by without noticing the need for a slight turn to avoid a pothole down the road. This group's lack of vision about what's coming—or what's possible—makes work into a stressful experience.

The Stress-Reward Endorphin Cycle

In order to circumvent the effects of stress on learning, it is important to understand exactly how deeply it is wired into us and why we become addicted to it.

Endorphins are chemicals in the brain that, when released, make us feel relaxed and happy. Not surprisingly, our bodies have learned to use these chemicals after we engage in activities that promote our most essential mission in life—survival. Endorphins are released when we eat, quench our thirst, have sex, and give birth to our children. We also get an endorphin release when we move our bodies, laugh, collaborate with others, and escape from danger (Wolfe, 2001; Berridge & Kringelbach, 2008; Kringelbach, 2008; Kringelbach, 2004).

Anyone reading this book can probably relate to the good feelings associated with these endorphin-releasing activities. When we narrowly avoid a car accident, we may feel a jittery euphoria, a response that's designed to reward our success and encourage us to remain vigilant in the future. Since these automated response mechanisms can't tell the difference between psychological and physical fear, we're likely to feel that same endorphin rush when we avoid (or survive) an uncomfortable meeting or finally finish a big job.

Is this a problem? Some scientists have argued that our bodies were not made to go into these metabolic states of danger-stress-response as often as psychological stress demands (Romero & Butler, 2007). If endorphins are released for surviving perceived danger or stress, over time this sets up a pattern of rewarding stress. Given the stress levels at some schools, one might experience an endorphin rush almost constantly—without ever having to run from a lion! As a result of this phenomenon, some organizations develop the rather odd relationship with psychological stress referred to in this text as the *stress-reward endor-phin cycle* (fig. 3.1). We experience a signal that resembles stress, grap-ple with it, perhaps amplify its meaning by sharing it, and then, when the stress reaches a certain level and we survive it, we get our silent endorphin reward.

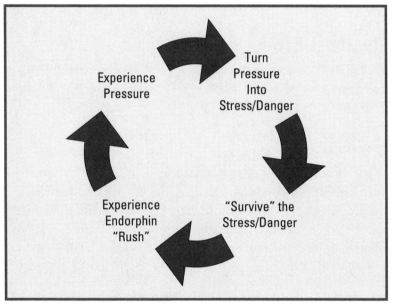

Figure 3.1: The stress-reward endorphin cycle.

The stress-reward endorphin cycle can help us understand why stress seems so persistent and why so many of us relive stressful experi-ences again and again with anyone who will listen: on some level, we are seeking the endorphin reward.

Solutions in Action: Interrupting the Cycle

The endorphin release can act as a kind of emotional junk food for the brain, and as with junk food, the short-term bliss we feel from a momentary escape can have high costs later. This insidious cycle rewards us in a way that undermines our growth efforts in school. Schools that get in the habit of seeking stress will find more of it, and the collective organizational learning will suffer.

Following are a number of effective strategies learning leaders can use to interrupt the cycle.

Apply the Change, Analysis, and Reframing Strategy

Sometimes we can interrupt the stress-reward cycle very quickly with the simple application of the change, analysis, and reframing strategy (page 33). For example, while attending a schoolwide meeting, the staff heard the district's new curriculum director, Dr. Snyder, say with a smile, "I've taken a look at the school's summer reading list. Clearly, we've got to make some changes to it!" Because there were other issues to address at the meeting, the summer reading list was not brought up again.

The next day several of the school's most prominent stress dealers discussed Dr. Snyder's comment and suggested that danger was just around the corner. They claimed teacher autonomy and academic freedom were on the ropes and further censorship would soon follow. In some schools, an offhand comment like this followed by perseverating stress dealers pushing their wares will inspire athletic leapfrogging from one conclusion to another. While the stress dealer makes apocalyptic predictions, however, a veteran of the change, analysis, and reframing strategy gathers all the necessary information. In this case, the simplest and most logical thing to do was to call Dr. Snyder and ask about his comment in order to establish whether or not it would have the grave consequences for the summer reading list that everyone was anticipating.

Even if Dr. Snyder had designs on making major changes in the district's purchase cycles for early elementary literature, gathering all the information up front (step one), analyzing the potential best- and worst-case scenarios (step two), and then identifying opportunities and reframing potentially negative consequences (step three) would give everyone a greater sense of empowerment and reduce stress overall. Most stress dealers enjoy the power they yield by ramping up the emotions of others and become profoundly discouraged by this level of thoughtful reaction and reflection. Weighing stress dealers down with facts and productive action discourages their efforts.

As it turned out, Dr. Snyder had money to allocate toward a teacher-led expansion of the reading list. By applying the strategy quickly, the team avoided analyzing only the worst-case scenario and thereby initiating another stress-reward response.

Engage in Healthy Endorphin Pursuits

We can also avoid the stress-reward endorphin cycle by creating endorphin-releasing activities that don't involve surviving danger. Fresh air, food and drink, social contacts, sunshine, and movement are all easily accessible endorphin stimulants (Cahill, 2000).

Carol and Deb were English teachers in Ohio in a large high school. After their teaching day was over, they would go for a power walk together in the hallways around the school. Soon, others would join them, and they found that by being together, moving, laughing, and getting some air, they were able to feel great after school and, at times, resolve issues that appeared to be insurmountable.

When we have healthy alternatives to the stress-reward endorphin cycle, jumping on that stress cycle seems less appealing and may help minimize the influence of those budding stress dealers.

Control Imitation and Stress Dialogue

Another way thoughtful learning leaders can manage stress is to establish a culture that limits the amount of stress imitation and stress dialogue in school.

As we have seen, human beings have a strong instinct to learn by observing and imitating the behavioral patterns of those around them (Meltzoff, 2007). Leaders at all levels need to be conscious of the degree to which their behaviors in any way celebrate stress. When leaders wear their stress as a badge of honor, it sends a message that stress is to be valued and that others should imitate their lead. Judy, the assistant principal from the beginning of this chapter who died on the job, spoke with an odd mix of angst and affection about the ever-growing mountain of paperwork on her desk and the line of recalcitrant teens at her door. Many of us are guilty at times of relishing the obstacles we face as a sign of the sacrifices we make and therefore our value. Judy had a number of colleagues who were happy to maintain the stress dialogue by vividly describing the crushing weight of their responsibilities and the dangers and impenetrable psyche of "today's kids."

Schools must be careful not to constantly engage in stress dialogue. Instead of talking about fears and problems, the best strategy is to speak to challenges and solutions. Being vigilant about the words we use and the actions we take will help support the spread of learning over the promulgation of stress.

Apply Positive Denial

When individuals or groups adamantly push back against an apparently negative set of outcomes or consequences, they are using *positive denial*. Positive denial focuses on opportunities and potential positive outcomes without denying the reality of the situation. For example, people diagnosed with cancer may use positive denial to focus more on the possibilities for healing than on the life-threatening and negative aspects of their condition (Barnett, 2006; Lazarus, 1998). A number of researchers say that positive denial can keep morale up, reduce anxiety, and prevent individuals or groups from becoming preoccupied with minor problems at the expense of long-term essential goals (Barnett, 2006; Friedel, Cortina, Turner, & Midgley, 2007; Lazarus, 1998).

Positive denial is similar to optimism, and psychologists have shown that individual and collective optimism has psychological advantages. Optimists, for example, tend to maintain internal and external dialogues in which they are hopeful regarding events in their life (Jacobs, 2003). According to Jacobs, by remaining optimistic, individuals and groups also acquire an increased sense of confidence.

In many organizations, being optimistic is seen as being unrealistic. Thoughtful learning leaders should work to extinguish this characterization and reward optimists for being serious contributors to deeper learning through the reduction of stress. Like other emotions, optimism can spread through imitation.

Promote Faith and Trust

Faith and trust are not easy to measure. These abstract concepts usually relate to deeply held personal beliefs. However, it's important to recognize their implications for managing stress. Compared to the statistical average, people who consistently practice their faith in a community setting tend to be happier and experience less stress-related illness, stroke, heart disease, and cancer (Steffen & Masters, 2005). They also have lower blood pressure and fewer heart attacks. The connection with faith appears to be one of the best predictors of overall life satisfaction (Koenig, McCullough, & Larson, 2001; Lipton, 2008).

There also appears to be a correlation between spirituality, faith and trust, and physical responses to stress, including cholesterol rates. People with these characteristics are less likely to be smokers, and several studies have indicated that they develop stronger immune systems (Koenig, McCullough, & Larson, 2001). They have also demonstrated an improved capacity to deal with bereavement, divorce, unemployment, and serious illness (Myers, 2000). Finally, individuals with greater levels of spirit and faith who become gravely ill appear to experience less pain and discomfort (Ebersohn, Maree, & Maree, 2006; Yates, Chalmer, St. James, Follansbee, & McKegney, 1981). In fact, simply viewing life as meaningful, either individually or as a group, helps to reduce the impact of stress (Jacobs, 2003).

Leaders can promote the virtues of faith and trust by believing that together they can meet the profound and awe-inspiring challenges that await them each day in school. These challenges can have huge consequences. For example, getting a struggling third-grade English language learner to start reading fluently might mean the difference between success or continued generational poverty for a family. Faith and trust are also demonstrated in the act of cooperation itself—by having faith in others and in believing they can be trusted.

The capacity for trust also appears to improve overall well-being and reduce stress. When human beings recognize signs of trust in those around them, their brains release endogenous oxytocin, a substance that apparently promotes relaxation. In other words, when we come together with people we trust, the brain tells us to relax (Zak, Borja, Kurzban, & Matzner, 2005). This is another confirmation by recent research of what many seminal leadership scholars have intuitively suspected: faith and trust are of paramount importance in leadership. Gregory Burns, in his book *Leadership* (1978), emphasized the importance of building connections and trust en route to developing a more transformational leadership platform, one that allows for transcendent growth and improvement. W. Edwards Deming, creator of the concept of total quality management, preached the importance of trust in developing high-functioning, self-governing, authentic organizations (Cobb, 2003). Today, hard science is supporting their legacy (Frese, 2008).

Establish Control and Empowerment

There is nothing worse for a powerful person than to suddenly feel powerless. If a dedicated group of teachers has worked for years to establish a highly effective literacy strategy, only to have that program eliminated without prior notification by their board of education, it's likely they will feel quite stressed and angry—they have lost control over their environment.

Thoughtful learning leaders must work diligently to give individuals and groups within the organization as much voice, control, and responsibility as possible over their working environment. Of the three, responsibility may be the one area we are neglecting the most in schools. Over the last twenty-five years, some well-intentioned school leaders have allowed other staff members to have a voice and to make decisions without any accountability for the results. While principals and central office leaders may think they are alleviating stress by not sharing the burden of accountability, they are in fact doing the opposite. Accountability on multiple levels in organizations has been shown over time to actually yield better results (Preuss, 2003). This is why financial gurus, for example, have always believed that virtual investing exercises are never as valuable as learning to invest with real money on the line.

Acknowledge the Inevitability of Change

We respond with stress to any change to our environment that threatens to interrupt our sense of balance, equilibrium, or well-being. Yet our approaches to instruction, the needs of our children, the content we teach, and almost everything else about our work in schools will be shaped and molded again and again throughout our careers. Change is a normal, inevitable, stimulating, and healthy aspect of what we do, and we can reframe issues to reflect that awareness. A more consistent acknowledgement of this can be beneficial in reducing stress. Instead of debating whether or not we should change, the more appropriate and empowering question is, "How and what should we change?"

Commit to Nurturing Social Ties

Social ties have a positive influence on reducing stress (Cacioppo, Hughes, Waite, Hawkley, & Thristed, 2006) and have even been known to reduce morbidity and mortality (Berkman & Glass, 2000). Social ties reduce isolation, inspire the confidence that's necessary to overcome formidable challenges, reduce distraction, and ultimately create deeper levels of learning.

Stress is an extremely powerful and omnipresent emotion, and it exists in our schools in plentiful supply. In this chapter, we have explored how stress often emerges as a result of miniscule amounts of fear that chip away at our psyche. We have looked at the power of the stress-reward cycle and the fact that, neurologically speaking, we may at times find ourselves obsessed with making stress a part of our working environment. The strategies recommended in this chapter can minimize stress and remove the hindrances to learning that it creates.

Stress can never be entirely eliminated, but thoughtful learning leaders can evaluate the strategies available to them to both acknowledge its presence and reduce its impact in school.

CHAPTER 4

Vision With Learning in Mind

Leaders lacking vision don't know where they're going, don't know how long the trip will take, and probably wouldn't recognize the destination even if they arrived by accident. Leaders with vision anticipate opportunities and challenges and share that vision in order to stimulate others to join them on the journey. The most inspirational leaders work collaboratively with staff members to construct, refine, and continuously reconstruct the collective vision of the school.

While honesty is the most desirable leadership characteristic, vision is often seen as a close second (Kouzes & Posner, 2009). From an evolutionary standpoint, our ancestors learned to follow leaders who had the wisdom to avoid danger and recognize opportunity. We arguably value vision so much because it also ties into issues of safety and emotional security: honest leaders with vision keep the pathway safe enough to allow for innovation and deep levels of learning.

Although vision is an intangible and elusive leadership quality, it's one that's necessary for any school. Just as an artist "sees" a masterpiece before ever picking up his chisel or brush, a leader or team of inspired leaders imagine unprecedented success, even in the face of low performance and previously unrecognized expectations. Teacher leaders with vision who are working with a struggling child can recognize deficiencies yet visualize interventions leading toward magnificent growth. A principal with true vision may see a school staff working in disconnected, idiosyncratic isolation and imagine a talented staff unleashed—collaborating and leading innovations like never before.

We tend to lionize leaders with vision. We credit them with an almost mystical clairvoyance and resist the notion that some of these skills are learned. However, vision doesn't have to be that rare and elusive, and it doesn't necessarily have to reside with leaders in a particular position. If we accept the basic assumption that leadership is a force within the organization that can be ignited, shared, and celebrated, then the construction of vision is available to anyone willing to step forth who is able to help shape and define it. A quiet voice doing humble work in the organization might step forth to lead an effort, clarify a destination, and identify a pathway toward the realization of that vision.

Today, the expansion of participation and access to information, along with ever-increasing diversity, gives us many alternative perspectives and approaches to choose from. This panorama will make us rich in the long run, but along the way it presents a number of challenges in establishing a collective sense of what's possible.

Core Knowledge: Vision Construction

The following is the learning leader's core knowledge regarding vision construction.

Seeing vs. Mental Representation

The world delivers a busy landscape to the eyes, and in an effort to make sense of it all, the brain makes choices about what is worth noticing in our field of vision. We tend to select things related to survivability along with things that have captured our interest due to our experiences, reflections, goals, and desires (Braine, 2009). Whatever our background, we will immediately notice a car driving off the road. But depending on who we are, our attention may or may not be drawn to country music, dreadlocks, or a new Mercedes-Benz.

Throughout life, the brain is engaged in an endless process of developing, examining, and continuously reshaping what we notice, based on our experiences. Those thought processes and systems of evaluation create within us a series of durable mental representations (Moss, Kotovsky, & Cagan, 2006). For example, you may meet someone and have a pleasant interaction. If, the next time you met, this person suddenly became violent and threatening toward you, your brain would quickly adjust that original mental representation. Were you to see that person again twenty years later, you would refer back to the more emotionally relevant of the two interactions.

Thus, we have a relatively static mechanical capacity to see the world around us. However, there are a number of internal and external variables that drive our construction of mental representations and therefore affect the way we make meaning out of what we see. Picture a wounded soldier lying in a hospital bed, being carefully tended by a nurse. In constructing that mental image, many of us would visualize a male being attended by a female—even though we know that a nurse can be a male and a soldier can be female. Our existing mental representations lead us in one direction or another.

From an organizational learning standpoint, vision refers to a collection of mental representations regarding a specific topic or idea. Since each person has different mental representations for the many concepts associated with the work we do as educators, pulling those multiple perspectives together around one vision is a very complex task.

The Role of Emotion and Belief

Emotion is at the heart of enduring mental representations—our emotions shape the mental representations we develop when we "see" (Gygax, Wagner-Egger, Parris, Seiler, & Hauert, 2008). The reason your grandfather still looks at your grandmother and sees a young bride in her early twenties has to do with the passion and love he felt for her when their eyes first met. Their initial encounter created an intense emotional response that led to a durable mental representation. When your grandfather tells you that his wife looks the same to him as she did fifty years earlier, he may not be exaggerating!

Our belief systems are also extremely important in the construction of mental representations. A teacher who believes that every child can learn and that a teacher's role is to serve will view a recalcitrant child differently than a teacher who believes some children need to be weeded out and that for others incarceration may be the only alternative. One teacher's belief system anticipates the emergence of high-performing leaders, while another's envisions orange jumpsuits and shackles.

The Role of Context

Context consists of the actual circumstance in which we find ourselves at the point a mental representation is introduced, constructed, or reshaped (Hall, 2007). Taking students who are studying civics to a court in session might provide an authentic context that will deepen their level of understanding of justice and the legal system. Context is the reason we propose to our future spouses in a romantic setting, decide to attend a football game with sixty thousand people rather than watch it on TV, and go to the library when studying for a test. Our learning context helps us to develop more durable mental representations and can help support mechanisms for recalling that information.

Leaders who are striving for greater clarity in collective vision, therefore, would not attempt to shape a new vision at a romantic restaurant or a football game. An awareness of context has led many leaders to take their teams off-site to plan or create.

Degree of Intention

The process of constructing a mental representation is also affected by what psychologists and brain researchers refer to as the *degree of intention* (Carrillat, d'Astous, & Colbert, 2008; Lee & Thorson, 2008). According to this phenomenon, what we construct as a mental image is driven by what we anticipate we will see. Before going into a collective bargaining session between teachers and the board of education, a participant might visualize clenched fists, red faces, divisive manipulations, and obscenity-laden verbal exchanges. Once there, he will look for confirmation of that vision. This outcome is even more likely to be actualized if leaders on both sides have this vision or expectation.

Degrees of intention differ from belief systems. Beliefs may be relatively static—we may believe that all children are good, but our degree of intention may lead us to anticipate a particular child's failure on a specific test. (That child may then surprise us and pass the test anyway.) Our belief systems are shaped by our values and can ultimately affect our degree of intention, but they are not the same.

Our degree of intention has a significant impact on our ability to establish, maintain, and reinforce our mental representations and, ultimately, our vision. That is why leaders can improve the vision construction process by sharing their degree of intention ahead of time. If a team has an overpowering expectation regarding the relative laziness of parents, the construction of a new parent-involvement plan will probably be affected by that. When team members share their degree of intention honestly, leaders and other members of the group can challenge these assumptions and improve the likelihood of a new and more empowering vision of change.

The Imprecision of Words

Historically, school leaders have relied largely on words to express their vision. A principal might give a speech at the beginning of the year that articulates his or her mental representations regarding change—some of them very complex—in order to shape an overall vision for the school. People sitting in the audience listening to the speech interpret these mental representations according to their beliefs, current learning context, and degrees of intention. Clearly, it is a huge leap of faith to assume that words alone can bridge this gap. Just as learning requires a number of authentic experiences over time, school leaders need to realize that the construction of a vision must be done strategically and through the exploration of shared learning experiences, not just words, over time. Words can help—but they cannot carry the day.

Mental Representations in Pre-K–12 Education

The following section identifies mental representations common to pre-K–12 education that learning leaders need to think about and challenge when attempting to drive change.

Mental Representations of Teachers

Are the teachers in your school seen as thoughtful, creative, heroic change agents or as frumpy, arbitrary rulemongers? Unfortunately, the entertainment industry bombards us constantly with antiquated and negative images of teachers. In its over twenty years on the air, *The Simpsons* has broadcast thousands of hours showing deeply flawed, frustrated, and cowardly teachers stumbling mightily at the obstacles set forth by Bart Simpson. More perplexing is that many teachers see themselves in this light. Clearly, frumpy rulemongers are not going to change the world. That is why schools should take steps to resist these negative stereotypes and reconstruct this mental representation.

Whenever possible, schools should portray teachers in the manner that best shows what they have to accomplish, and when teachers are being thoughtful, creative, or heroic their efforts should be put on display, thus creating a new mental representation.

Mental Representations of the Principal

Hollywood's interpretation of the role of the principal certainly isn't very flattering, either. Principals are often portrayed as petty, rule-obsessed, frustrated, and one-dimensional. In the wildly popular movie *Napoleon Dynamite* (Hess, 2004), the principal delivered a series of shallow misguided lectures to the students and was later shown anonymously leering at coeds. In *Ferris Bueller's Day Off* (Hughes, 1986), the shouting, disheveled, and frustrated principal was perfectly juxtaposed with Ferris, a cool, calm, and collected student. Despite these images, the reality is that most principals are well educated, talented, tireless—even heroic and inspiring. Once again, there is a generous chasm between these perspectives. The mental representations a school adopts regarding the position of principal are an important factor in how a principal's leadership is received. As with the mental representations of teachers, schools must take decisive steps to disavow these caricatures and present a contemporary vision of what it means to be a principal.

Mental Representations of Learning

Some schools regard learning as a process of discovering, nurturing, or harvesting undiscovered strengths. However, a more common mental representation is of the learner as an empty vessel waiting to be filled at the fountain of knowledge by the all-knowing teacher. Consistently constructing mental representations involving discovery or nurturing changes the way we interact with students and each other and the way we think about the essence of our work. Discovering inherent strengths is a very different vision of learning than filling an empty receptacle.

Mental Representations of Leadership

We have described leadership as a force driven collectively by emotion, energy, and will. It emerges from all corners an organization, and

Vision Statements, Mission Statements, and Mottos

Vision statements, mission statements, and mottos are designed to inform an audience about what the organization intends to accomplish so that the decisions people make along the way will be in keeping with the collective vision. They are not always successful. For years, Richard DuFour (2004) has been accurately pointing out how futile school mission statements can be. Many schools have a mission statement that either no one knows about or that contains meaningless platitudes and hyperbole that contribute little to the progress of the school.

Still, some mottos are quite effective and illuminating. Ask anyone who has been a soldier in the last fifty years about the motto *You never, ever leave a soldier behind.* The strategies may have changed since World War II, but the meaning behind those words remains relevant.

In the 2008 presidential campaign, Barack Obama was criticized for the simplicity of his message *Yes, we can.* At one point, his then main Republican rival, Rudolph Giuliani, presented Rudy's Twelve Commitments. Each commitment began with the phrase, *I will.* For example, *I will cut taxes and reform the tax code, I will reform the legal systems and appoint strict constructionist judges, I will keep America on the offense in the war on terror.* At a turning point in Giuliani's run for the Republican nomination, he gave a key speech on his twelve commitments. While walking off the stage, he quickly turned and ran back to the microphone—he had forgotten one of them (MSNBC, 2007). The simplicity of *Yes, we can* as compared to the complexity of a dozen commitments ultimately spoke to the electorate. Giuliani's use of the pronoun *I* in attempting to construct a vision was also much less powerful than President Obama's use of the word *we.* By building a vision that reinforced inclusiveness and a focus on others, the Obama campaign developed a unique set of mental representations associated with him and his journey to becoming president. His ability to use social networking sites and to market in the inclusive and highly interactive world of the Internet further reinforced the notion of *we,* while other candidates remained talking heads on television.

Between an emotionally resonant and meaningful motto and a mission statement that nobody knows or cares about, the former wins every time. By articulating a generalized vision of what's possible, a motto can bring people together, and that can be the first step toward accomplishing a great deal.

it is perhaps more powerfully illustrated by an artist's brush than a flow chart. Yet in some schools, mental representations regarding leadership almost always default to a specific position or person. These two mental representations—leadership as an organic force and leadership as a position—diverge dramatically. The degree to which a school is self-directed, creative, and emergent is driven to a great extent by the degree to which there is clarity about what leadership means—and what it doesn't mean.

Mental Representations of Change

A classic mental representation of change in schools might include an individual or group succumbing to the wishes of another individual or group. We also frequently represent change as episodic. A more contemporary vision of change represents it as a continuous state of evolution, growth, and improvement (Mohan, Peng, & Ramesh, 2008). If you see change as episodic, you can hide from it or wait until it's over; if you see change as a constant, hiding is not an option, and there is a greater likelihood that more comprehensive levels of engagement and participation will follow.

Solutions in Action: Developing Focused Mental Representations

The research-based perspectives in this chapter are probably aligned with what you have sensed all along about the art of leadership. That is why leaders who have studied the phenomenon of mental representation usually grasp the spirit of these concepts based on their own experience. The goal of this chapter is to make the process of identifying, articulating, clarifying, and sharing an organizational vision more accessible to leaders at all levels. Bringing what we know about this mental process to more people will help to realize the benefits of clear vision more widely.

Learning leaders can use the following nine-step protocol, which strategically applies what we've learned about mental representations, to create a clear and definable organizational vision. This protocol can be implemented quickly and informally with small groups or more formally when applied in a larger and more complex context.

Step One: Evaluating Personal Belief Systems

Our personal belief systems shape our actions and profoundly influence our vision of the world. It may take years of working on a team for its members to truly understand one another's closely held personal beliefs. With such an understanding, however, a team is much more likely to create a clear collective vision. Consideration of the formative statements listed in table 4.1 (and any others that the group may find useful) can serve as conversation starters and help clarify similarities and differences among team members' belief systems.

Table 4.1: Personal Belief System Evaluation Questions

Please mark your level of agreement with the following statements.

1   Strongly disagree
2   Disagree
3   Agree
4   Strongly agree

I am capable of producing truly outstanding results.	1	2	3	4
Our team is capable of producing truly outstanding results.	1	2	3	4
Our school as a whole has the capacity to produce truly outstanding results.	1	2	3	4
Our progress is determined to a great extent by our beliefs and actions.	1	2	3	4
The work we are doing here is important.	1	2	3	4

Visit **go.solution-tree.com/leadership** to download and print this resource.

These statements can reveal the limits of a team's beliefs. It is difficult to have a far-reaching vision regarding change if there is an overwhelming mental representation about the limits of what is possible.

When groups are evaluating their individual answers to these questions, watch out for the chorus of "if onlys" that may be inserted along the way. "*If only* the parents cared . . . " "*If only* we had a different principal . . . " "*If only* the union would not stand in our way . . . " Such statements imply that there are changes *others* need to make.

The following open-ended statements can also be excellent conversation starters when examining beliefs:

- "One strongly held belief I have regarding our work together is
  _____."

- "_____ has a profound impact on my beliefs regarding my work."

Once again, be mindful of strongly held beliefs that involve people other than the speaker growing, changing, or evolving. The most effective teams are led by individuals who, by adjusting their belief systems regarding their work, begin to open their minds to previously unimagined possibilities.

Having this conversation collaboratively allows those in the group with the brightest and most ambitious mental representations to express themselves and to potentially open others up to these possibilities. Forward-thinking learning leaders are always pushing the organization to expand the limits of what is possible.

Step Two: Evaluating Context

While beliefs tend to be relatively static, the context in which we work can ebb and flow rather dramatically in a short period of time. Thoughtful learning leaders understand that creating a focused mental representation requires an awareness of the impact of context and the ability to prevent contextual factors from derailing the process. To aid this process, consider the following context-related questions:

- "What five things have happened to us in the past in our school that affect our progress today as a group?"

- "What five things are going on in school today that will influence our work now and in the future?"

In response to these questions, teams might identify the recent failure of a tax levy, poor performance on state tests, the retirement of a popular teacher leader, or a dramatic reduction in budget as factors discouraging teachers and affecting their capacity to visualize a change outcome. Conversely, a recent victory or award, an unexpected accomplishment, or a remarkable elevation in performance might stimulate the entire organization and affect the energy, focus, and enthusiasm the group has when facing its challenges.

These conversations about context give the group perspective on factors that might influence their thinking. The ones with the greatest amount of emotional energy will make the greatest difference. Some, such as the death of a colleague or a major accomplishment, are impossible to ignore and will affect the learning context no matter what a team does.

Step Three: Evaluating Existing Mental Representations

As stated earlier, existing mental representations influence the construction of future vision. A high school math department that sees block scheduling as an insurmountable impediment will approach its change efforts differently than one that associates that concept with flexibility and opportunity. Therefore, it is essential to consider the dominant mental representations already in place. The following questions will support that discussion:

- "What are the dominant mental representations about the work we are currently doing?"

- "What other essential mental representations do we have about our school, our goals, and each other?"

Participants will gradually begin to differentiate the effects of belief systems, learning context, and existing mental representations on their work. At this point, team members may recognize that they have, for example, a generalized *belief* that all students can learn and that the team is capable of truly outstanding accomplishments by pulling together. They may recognize, too, that the *context* of their situation is discouraging—they have just gone through some budget cuts, and an exciting and helpful new teacher had to be let go. In addition to the discouraging contextual situation, they may recognize that their *mental representations* regarding their principal and the school improvement model they are using are both fairly negative and that these perspectives have permeated the group and are influencing its confidence in moving forward.

Step Four: Evaluating Current Degree of Intention

The concept of degree of intention relates to what we expect. When walking into a horror movie, we *expect* to be afraid. When going to our great aunt's home as a child, we anticipated that we would be bored. Our expectations, or *degree of intention,* are driven to a great extent by our belief systems, current learning context, and existing and evolving mental models. In evaluating this step in the process, consider the following questions:

- "What outcomes do we envision in relationship to the major work challenges facing this group?"

- "How do you see the group evolving in relationship to this vision of what is possible?"

These questions are designed to help groups become increasingly specific about identifying a vision they can share and pursue. If the first four steps of the process have been followed, it is likely at this point in the discussion that degrees of intention have begun to develop within the group.

Step Five: Establishing New Degrees of Intention

This step is designed to encourage group members to evaluate whether they have sufficiently challenged themselves with regard to what is possible—that is, to push back against any resistance and reach for greater degrees of intention. Consider the following questions and their implications:

- "What would our performance be like if we improved and evolved as a team well beyond expected levels?"

- "What great accomplishments are possible if we do better than we imagine?"

- "What specifically would that look like?"

At this point, the group should set aside the "yeah buts" and avoid getting bogged down by all the reasons why accomplishing the goal is impossible. Instead, it should use its collective intelligence to reach beyond what it had previously considered possible.

Step Six: Evaluating Current Belief Systems

At this point in the planning, it is helpful to go back and examine the belief statements articulated in steps one and two. For example, the group may have had a belief that the school's budget challenges represent an insurmountable obstacle to student achievement. After identifying a vision for goal attainment, the team may realize that putting that belief aside is going to be essential for goal attainment to become a reality. They may see that they have to focus on more empowering beliefs, such as "This team is capable of overcoming almost anything to make its goals a reality."

The following questions may help stimulate this conversation:

- "What beliefs do we have about ourselves and our team that we may need to change or reexamine in order to make our new collective vision come to fruition?"

- "What belief systems do we have about our school and profession that need to change in order to make our new collective vision come to fruition?"

Step Seven: Establishing New Actions to Support a New Vision

It is likely the team will now feel more optimistic about what is possible. Because of our natural learning rhythms, however, we tend to pay more attention to actions than words (Caine, Caine, McClintic, & Klimek, 2005). To prepare to run a marathon for the first time, a runner needs to evaluate his or her beliefs, establish empowering mental representations, and adjust his or her degree of intention; but at some point, all that thinking needs to result in action! Therefore, it is extremely important within this planning process that the team identify action steps it can implement immediately. This commitment to action will help the team realize that even its loftiest and most difficult goals are within reach. The following questions can help lead that conversation:

- "What actions must we take now or very soon in order to make this vision of outstanding performance become a reality?"

- "What actions must we take immediately in order to make this vision of outstanding performance a reality? What actions just can't wait?"

Step Eight: Reviewing the Learning Context

In general, the lower our levels of emotion or commitment, the more important context becomes. In other words, a team that is steadfastly determined to improve an otherwise difficult circumstance is much less likely to be deterred by context than a group that isn't clear about its goals and direction. In considering the issue of context, it is important to recognize that certain contextual variables simply cannot be controlled—for example, a school going broke, a staff member retiring or being laid off, or the community voting down a tax. However, the degree to which such factors derail the vision is, to a great extent, up to the group itself. A school that is passionately committed to its long-term goals and objectives will be less thrown by short-term contextual obstacles.

We are only human, and contextual factors will either support or negate our efforts. Using questions like the following, the team can thoughtfully evaluate the degree to which it is willing to allow external influences to shape its vision and control its accomplishments:

- "What good things are going on in school today that could add to our feelings of pride and joy?" Good news can have a positive impact on the learning context if those positive circumstances are known throughout the organization. For example, a teacher may be obtaining National Board certification, or the district may have just received a grant. One staff member may be getting a doctorate, or another may have become a grandparent.

- "What steps can we take to ensure these positive contextual factors are known throughout the school?" While bad news travels fast, the best learning organizations find a way to share good news quickly as well. What systems does the school currently have in place for sharing good news? Al Widner, a long-term superintendent in Michigan, is famous for always finding a way in his correspondence to share what he calls his "points of pride." Recognizing and celebrating positive contextual factors that improve learning is essential to reshaping vision.

- "What steps can we take to mitigate the influence of negative contextual factors?" For this question, teams should explore mechanisms for addressing factors that diminish the learning context. The death of a teaching colleague, for example, could have an enormous impact on the learning context in any school. Not dealing with that death appropriately, for example by giving people time to grieve and reach out to those around them, could be distracting and debilitating. One effort a team can make in this area is to create a team that's ready to deal with these types of issues when they arise.

Step Nine: Continuously Reexamining the Vision

Our vision of our work, ourselves, and each other is always evolving. Furthermore, that vision is being continually challenged by ongoing shifts in our mental representations, beliefs, context, and degrees of intention. Thoughtful learning leaders must, therefore, constantly push the organization to evaluate and reestablish a clear vision for their work. The larger and more complex the organization, the more strategic the process of re-examining the vision must be. The following questions may help a team with this step:

- "What steps can we take to regularly revisit the construction of our vision?"

- "Are there points in our annual, quarterly, monthly, weekly, or daily processes in which we could infuse examination of our vision in order to maintain more focus?"

Again, it is important to remember that this nine-step process can be used on either a large scale or with a relatively small group. Once the team has experienced working with the steps, it can more quickly evaluate the relevance of context, disempower old mental representations, and more strategically identify the influences that shape their work.

※

By evaluating vision from the standpoint of individual and collective learning, we can ensure that we do not take vision for granted. This process also helps us avoid the often mistaken assumption that others can picture in their minds what we have been attempting to express. As we become aware of the mental representations, beliefs, degrees of intention, and contexts present in a group, we can reconcile them so that they all ultimately contribute to the new vision. The establishment of such a new and compelling vision can dramatically influence the emotional energies of the change process in a school. Nothing is more powerful than a group of motivated, compassionate adults who have come together with a clear vision of what is possible and can combine their efforts and energies toward attaining it. They will achieve what others see as out of reach.

Purpose-Driven Inquiry

Questions improve engagement and form connections between previous knowledge and current learning content (Marquardt, 2004). Questions also stimulate team learning. Given our propensity as a species to gather in groups or tribes and share our emotional states, it's not surprising that collective inquiry pursuits are quite common in organizational settings (Preskill & Catsambas, 2006). It has been said that inquiry is to organizations what sunlight is to plants (Coulter, 2006).

Why do some organizations ask better questions than others? If a school staff finds out that test results were far lower than expected, that school will collectively begin to reflect on the news. One school might ask, "Why are the tests so difficult?" "Is there some problem with our students?" "What's wrong with the principal?" Another school might respond to the same results by asking, "What can we do to come together, grow, and change in the name of making things better for these students?" The questions we ask shape our actions and can significantly impact our experiences. Every generation approaches the future with questions. The dramatic shifts in how we work, learn, and interact brought about by fast-moving technology and cultural change have made asking the right questions more important than ever for leaders trying to shape the world around them.

Core Knowledge: Inquiry

Let's look at our core knowledge regarding why inquiry works, how it works, and what effect it has on learning leadership.

Questions Have Always Been the Answer

Inquiry has the capacity to create a perpetual inner dialogue. Inner dialogue is mainly carried on through the stories people tell themselves

and each other to justify their interpretations of events and their decisions (Busche & Kassam, 2005). This capacity to maintain an inner dialogue is a unique feature of the human condition. Throughout humanity's
journey, we have used our power to ask and reflect on seminal questions to guide our existence. Asking, "How can I improve my shelter?"
for over a thousand generations has led us beyond simply taking care
of ourselves to creating the highly sophisticated domiciles we call home
today. Virtually everything we know, experience, or enjoy has evolved
over time, thanks to the power of asking the right questions. Inquiry has
been the inspiration for revolution, war, and the technological break-
throughs that kept our ancestors alive during tough times. In a sense,
the exponential growth of the Internet has been driven to a great extent
by our desire to ask questions and share our answers with each other.

Inquiry Resides Between Emotion and Action

As we have already seen, emotional impulses get our attention and
stimulate our learning systems (Barrett, 2007; Paz, Pelletier, Bauer, &
Pare, 2006). Emotions also create within us a sense of urgency about formulating a plan of action; in some circumstances, emotion can drive us
to immediate action. However, when we make time for reflection, the
questions we shape can determine the actions we take. Every staff in
every school feels emotion and takes action, but the questions they ask
in between matter just as much.

Inquiry Is a Collective Pursuit

Our emotions are magnified when we are in a group. Furthermore,
when we're together we attempt to bring our emotional states into congruence. If you walk into a room and a group of ten people are angry,
sad, happy, or excited, it is difficult not to feel the tug of those dominant
emotions and the desire to align with them (Stout, 2007). This emotional commonality also affects our inquiry pursuits. Our tribal tendency to be drawn together emotionally conditions what we focus on,
ask about, and do (Cooperrider, Whitney, & Stavros, 2003). Clear and
focused questions empower individuals in groups to learn much more
collectively than they would working alone (Whitney & Trosten-Bloom,
2003; Reason & Reason, 2006)—all the more reason to be thoughtful
and strategic about our collective inquiry pursuits.

How You State the Question Matters

We know today that the language we use in creating inquiry pursuits has a dramatic effect on the focus and direction of our learning (Trosten & Bloom, 2003). Inspiring military leaders, coaches, and other icons of leadership have always asked tough and thought-provoking questions of those around them. John F. Kennedy used a carefully crafted question to inspire a country to service: "Ask not what your country can do for you, ask what you can do for your country." On the other hand, it is not uncommon to see the power of language influencing inquiry patterns and learning in a negative way. Individuals who are obsessed with questions like "What's wrong with them?" "Why don't things ever go right in school?" and "Why can't they stop complaining?" lead groups toward pursuits that are uninspiring at best and, at worst, destructive to the growth trajectory of the organization. The following are ineffective inquiry patterns that are often found in learning organizations.

Profound Incuriosity

Some schools develop a pattern of acting as if they aren't passionate about any pursuit at all. *What if* questions are met more often than not with "So what?" These schools become frustrated with unanswered questions and feel the need to quickly bring their pursuits to fruition, even when the issues are extremely complex. Being incurious in these schools is viewed, absurdly, as a sign of strength: since they have all the answers, there's no need to wonder about anything. In reality, incurious organizations are often fearful ones. They lack the confidence to pursue questions because they don't believe they'll find the answers, even if they make the effort. They have found over time that it is easier to put up a visage of incuriosity than to fall short. The problem with being profoundly incurious, of course, is that as the world continues to change and evolve, these organizations fall further and further behind.

Fervent Faultfinding

Some organizations, particularly those in toxic environments, find fault whenever possible—in the teachers, students, administration, community, government, or the profession as a whole. Finding fault isn't very difficult, and schools that adopt this inquiry pattern are setting a very low standard. Schools that are struggling mightily typically know all too well where their faults lie, but spending time asking and answering questions about existing faults is arguably much easier than taking the time necessary to identify strategies that might make a difference. Thoughtful leaders from throughout the organization should be ready to generate important organizational questions—but those questions are not about finding fault.

Seeking the Status Quo

Some schools constantly find themselves asking and answering questions that lead right back to the current situation. This pattern may be driven by a deeply held intention to maintain and promote the cultural standard that already exists in the school, the community, or both. Groups that seek to preserve the status quo often do so out of a wish for certainty or comfort. When we watch a movie that we enjoy more than once, we may be looking to repeat a familiar, positive experience. Schools seeking the status quo are perhaps doing the same thing.

Deliberate Derailment

Some groups, realizing the power of inquiry to capture our attention, drive action, and maintain our focus, try to establish an agenda that derails the progress of others. For example, a small but focused group of leaders may have a vision for driving change at a very deep level, in a way that would require teachers and administrators to reconceptualize their efforts, work harder, and move out of their comfort zone. Rather than being inspired by this vision, groups uninterested in change may dramatically pose questions that are emotionally disproportionate to the situation in order to create intensity and distraction—questions like "What if the new plan results in mass layoffs?" and "What if we can't afford it?" and "What if we get overwhelmed?" and "Aren't we already overworked?" Derailing-type questions may sometimes become personal, gratuitously calling into question the motives and integrity of the change agents themselves.

Trained Not to Ask

Circus elephants used to endure humiliating and cruel training protocols. Their keepers tied chains to their feet when they were very young and beat them to instill fear and convince them it was futile to try to escape. When an elephant grew up, it could still be held in place by those same chains, even though they were hardly a match anymore for its enormous strength. Just like the elephant that outgrew its chains, many schools today have immense collective power that is limited only by a belief in their weakness. We also have a legacy of teachers and principals who use fear and intimidation as a primary mechanism of control. Groups under the sway of these individuals don't pursue inspiring questions, because the answers they might elicit, or even the pursuit itself, would give the group strength and authority their "trainers" had not planned on.

Types of Questions Your School Should Ask

Inquiry shapes emotional focus in our work and gives us the impetus to take direct action. If we do not ask empowering and focused questions, we will not achieve the results we desire. The following types of questions, when used on a consistent basis, are likely to lead to focused pursuits and profound results.

Ownership-Oriented Questions

Schools that are unsuccessful often get involved with inquiry pursuits regarding variables or outcomes over which they have no control. Questions like "Why do we have to make up snow days?" and "Why do so many of our kids come from broken homes?" are examples of inquiry pursuits concerning issues the inquirer doesn't own. On the other hand, when we feel ownership over outcomes, we ask questions like "How can we change that?" and "How can I make a difference?" and "How can we identify and implement a solution to that problem?"

The best ownership-oriented inquiry pursuits involve questions we ourselves ask, answer, and ultimately are accountable for. If we're allowed to ask questions that others own, we aren't as likely to be as concerned about what answering that question actually means.

We Questions

The most successful schools consistently frame their inquiry pursuits around the pronoun *we*. Rather than talking about what *he* or *she* is doing, or what *I* need, these schools constantly think about their challenges from a team or group perspective, knowing that profound answers come this way. Challenges are also much less stressful and frustrating when we face them together. If we face a difficult challenge in school, isn't it less stressful to ask, "How are we going to handle this?" rather than silently wondering in solitude, "What am I going to do?!"

Courageous and Motivating Questions

Although we may take a certain pleasure in the certainty that comes with asking and answering easy questions, the brain was made to be challenged. Great schools don't inspire their creative genius by asking, "What can we do to raise our scores by 1 percent?" or "What steps can we take to *slightly* improve student achievement?" The best organizations ask bold, even outrageous questions like "Who says our school can't be one of the best in the state?" and "Why do our kids have to continue a tradition of failure and poverty after graduation?" Courageous questions will likely bring criticism, but the most profound results in schools have come as the result of dedicated teams being willing to ask questions that must at first have seemed outlandish to their critics.

The happiest schools are teeming with staff members who constantly ask themselves difficult, motivating questions.

Specific and Direct Questions

Successful schools don't spend time in the ivory tower contemplating theories, and they don't chase ghosts. They identify clear, focused, understandable inquiry pursuits. "How can we help our current underperforming migrant population meet or exceed state standards and dramatically reduce the rate at which they drop out?" is a specific, answerable question that goes well beyond whimsically wondering, "What are we going to do about those poor kids who move around all the time?"

Temporarily Unanswered Questions

We have a tendency in our work in schools to rush to an answer when we hear an uncomfortable silence after a question. However, thoughtful, successful schools learn to become comfortable with the sound of silence after a question is asked. Some questions in an organization take an extended period of time to answer, while the adults take time to think through thoughtful, strategic answers. Being comfortable with the sense of incompletion that goes with pondering a question for days, weeks, or months takes discipline and foresight.

Obvious Questions

Being willing to ask the obvious questions is one of the best things a school can do. Schools that have developed a degree of psychological safety and a willingness to learn and grow aren't afraid to seek clarification by asking "I don't know what you mean" or "I am completely confused. Let's start again." A reframing question that may appear to take the group back a few steps may be necessary in a group that's striving to improve. Asking such questions can help create a sense of safety, or it might clear up lingering misconceptions about a concept. Even more, it can avert serious mistakes.

The Challenger and the Titanic

The *Titanic* sank on April 14, 1912, and the *Challenger* space shuttle exploded on January 28, 1986. Even though there were seventy-four years between these tragedies, there was one marked similarity. Analysis of the planning and engineering in both situations revealed that group members working on both the ocean liner and the space shuttle had serious concerns regarding engineering and program design. Yet in both cases, the engineers hesitated to bring up these concerns out of fear of looking ignorant or misinformed (Marquardt, 2004). Certainly, both of these tragedies should remind us that it is better to ask a "dumb" question than to sit silently while mistakes are being made.

Questions That Inspire Curiosity

The best questions stimulate deeper levels of curiosity. This is why it is so important to ask deep, profound, and—at times—difficult questions of ourselves regarding our work in schools—for example, "Could preventing early learning failure in our pre-K and early elementary program cut our special education rate in half by the time those students are in middle school?" The question of how to help hundreds of students overcome learning failure at a young age might make a learning team intensely curious about finding an answer.

Solutions in Action: Purpose-Driven Inquiry

This section presents a six-step protocol for a purpose-driven team inquiry. This protocol can help identify current inquiry patterns and reframe them in ways that lead to more productive transitions from emotion to question to action. It can be used in small groups or with the entire staff, and for modest projects as well as for overarching school improvement planning.

Step One: Identifying the Question and Knowing Why We Ask It

For step one of this process, groups will be asked to identify the types of questions they find themselves constantly asking and answering. Since most schools don't consciously identify the inquiry pursuits in which they are already involved, refer to tables 5.1 and 5.2 (page 80) for lists of effective and ineffective questions that might dominate an inquiry agenda. Table 5.1 lists questions related to school improvement and organizational learning.

Having provided this list of questions a number of times in schools in the United States and other countries, I am never surprised to see the most successful schools asking questions from the effective column.

In examining the ineffective column, it's clear that a number of these inquiry pursuits lack ownership and are faultfinding. For example, teachers and principals can't own the problem regarding community values or the beliefs of the superintendent and school board. That is why there is often no requisite action to take in reference to the ineffective questions, except to continue asking the unanswerable.

Schools that have been resolutely pursuing negative, disempowering, and ineffective questions for decades have become expert at finding fault with principals, diagnosing what's wrong with parents and students, and pointing out maladies in each other and the community. Unfortunately, doctoral degrees aren't issued for this sort of skill, nor does this pursuit lead to anything except a toxic environment and underperformance. Almost no one in these organizations ever asks, "What can we do to help the new principal be successful?" or "How can we support the teachers in their need to feel empowered and connected?" or "What can we do to demonstrate our value to the community?"

Table 5.1: Purpose-Driven Inquiry—Questions About Process

Ineffective	Effective
1. Why aren't parents more involved?	1. How can we make parents feel welcome?
2. Why doesn't the community value what we do?	2. How can we show the community we value them?
3. What's wrong with our principal?	3. What support does the principal need from us?
4. What's wrong with our teachers?	4. What needs do the teachers have?
5. What's wrong with the superintendent and school board?	5. How can we support the superintendent or school board?
6. Why won't my colleague just do his job?	6. What does my colleague need from me? From us?
7. How soon can I retire?	7. What more can I do?
8. Where's the party?	8. Where's the next challenge?
9. What's wrong with us?	9. What are our strengths? How can we capitalize on them?
10. What's wrong with you?	10. What are my strengths? How can I capitalize on them?
11. What's wrong with me?	11. What can I do to help?
12. What if we fail?	12. How can we perform beyond expectations?
13. Why are we so poorly funded?	13. How can we get the funding that we need?

Visit **go.solution-tree.com/leadership** to download and print this resource.

Taking the focus off negative pursuits doesn't mean that problems don't exist. Indeed, the principal really may be ineffective, or a group of teachers may be obstructionists. Perhaps the students actually *are* out of control and the community is going through a very difficult transition;

but unless the question is designed to be a cathartic shout to the stars, the best answers to these challenges won't come by continually highlighting them.

Some schools find themselves constantly focused on questions relating to retirement, vacation, or the next social gathering. They may be bored or preoccupied, or just be nervous in the face of a difficult challenge. It's easier to ponder questions about what you'll do when you stop working than it is to face the immediate challenges of a complex situation.

Table 5.2: Purpose-Driven Inquiry—Questions About Students and Learning

Ineffective	Effective
1. What's wrong with these students?	1. How can we more comprehensively support our students?
2. How can I get the students to learn this content?	2. How can we facilitate our students' learning journey?
3. How can I get through this content in an hour?	3. How can this material be presented in a way that facilitates deep learning?
4. Why are our students so distracted?	4. How can we help our students find focus?
5. Why don't students care?	5. How can we motivate the students to learn?
6. Why don't students do their homework?	6. Is homework necessary? If so, what's the purpose?
7. Why are the students' skills so underdeveloped?	7. How can we enhance the skills we have?

Visit **go.solution-tree.com/leadership** to download and print this resource.

Notice that in table 5.2, which lists common inquiry pursuits related to students and learning in pre-K–12 education, the lack of ownership in the list of effective questions has disappeared. Even though several of the questions use the pronoun *I*, the actions themselves largely refer to the efforts of a group. Each question, instead of being a cleverly disguised way of complaining, points to some empowering action. It's clear that the responses to the ineffective and effective lists would drive a school in two very different directions.

Sometimes even a well-intentioned question can lead us in the wrong direction. For example, question number two asks, "How can I get the students to learn this content?" Here, the teacher sees herself as working alone ("How can *I . . .*"). A better question would be, "How can we facilitate their learning journey?" In some cases, a shift of emphasis like that can be more important than the student's learning a prescribed amount of content. A student who is profoundly at risk may improve tremendously by working with a particular teacher, while not yet performing in any way close to the state standard. In such cases, asking how much the student *grew* is far more representative of the progress of both the teacher and the student than simply asking how the student performed with regard to an external measurement.

Asking, "How can I get through this content in an hour?" focuses a teacher on increasing his or her efficiency—it's a question that assumes the best way to measure effectiveness is by considering the variable of time. Time constraints may very well be an important variable, but a well-intentioned team of teachers who are passionately pursuing the goal of time efficiency may neglect to look hard enough at the impact they are having on student achievement.

Some schools become obsessed with questions like "Why don't students do their homework?" or "What can we do to get the students to turn their homework in on time?" Yet when they examine these questions more thoroughly, they are not sure *why* they spend so much time obsessing on them. In an era when so many students have disconnected home lives, homework is sometimes more of an exercise in agility than responsibility (Margolis, 2005).

By the end of this step in the process, teams will have identified questions that are being implicitly or explicitly asked and answered in the school that are worth pursuing, either individually or collectively. This discussion may also yield a number of questions that are not on this list.

Step Two: Igniting Collective Curiosity

Curiosity breeds a sense of fun, innovation, and excitement, and those good feelings bring out the best in us. By addressing problems together, teams address the hindrance of fear and are inspired and energized to work at their creative best, often igniting an individual and collective genius that has been waiting to emerge.

The objective of this step is to root out ineffective questions and to identify and clarify those more passionate pursuits related to the emotional intentions of the organization. It is also important here to look judiciously at the number of questions being considered, since schools typically cannot make progress on too many inquiry pursuits at once. Schools should be strategic and identify inquiry pursuits that could potentially make a big difference in the overall growth of the organization. Here, once again, we are engaging the power of emotion to bring energy and focus to the work. To complete step two, consider the following questions:

- "Which questions do we feel most passionately about? What is it about this pursuit that is so important to us?"

- "What emotions do we feel in relationship to the pursuit of these questions?"

- "From a goal-attainment standpoint, does the pursuit of these questions yield results in our most important areas? Are we asking questions that give us the best bang for our buck?"

By asking these questions following the discussion about effective and ineffective questions, it's likely that a thoughtful dialogue will ensue, one that can shine a light on inquiry patterns helpful to the work of the team and questions that should be reshaped or retired altogether. By identifying more effective, profound, and focused inquiry pursuits and by paying careful consideration when formulating them to word choice and syntax, teams will have a greater focus and direction. Just as importantly, however, these strategic discussions around inquiry pursuits are likely to engage the individual and collective emotional energies of the team and develop one of the most underdiscussed but powerful forces for learning: curiosity.

Ideally, at the end of this step, the team can move forward with a set of inquiry pursuits that its members feel passionate about.

Step Three: Defining Strategic Action

In step one, the team had an honest conversation about questions that are being consistently asked and answered. In step two, the team evaluated the questions that are currently receiving the highest levels of priority, the emotions that are associated with them, and the degree to which this pattern of asking and answering these questions is actually paying dividends for the school. If your team decided that too many of these questions are ineffective, your goal should then be to seek an inquiry pattern that is more effective and fluid. Step three of the process will help the group to make this transition. By formulating answers to the following questions, the team will begin to see an effective inquiry agenda beginning to emerge:

- "Are our inquiry pursuits worded in an effective, proactive manner consistent with the recommendations in this chapter?" In thinking about wording, consider whether the questions are ownership oriented. Are they *we* questions? Are they courageous and motivating, specific and direct?

- "Does this inquiry pursuit require additional strategic planning? If so, when are we getting started, and who will lead the charge?" Often teams or entire schools will spend years asking important questions but get so caught up in the hypnosis of their day-to-day work they neglect to take steps toward actually finding answers to them.

- "What specific steps must we take immediately to pursue this topic? Who is responsible for taking these steps, and how soon will they get started?" Once again, these are empowering questions that help a team get specific about actions.

- "What supports will be needed to pursue these topics, and where can these supports be found? Who's responsible for identifying them, and how soon will they begin?" This additional detail moves the team toward a more formalized strategic planning process. Depending on the question and the challenges ahead, more or less planning may be required.

- "How high are the stakes regarding this inquiry pursuit? How can we make the case that pursuing this question is worth the priority it has been given?" This question helps to reinforce the emotions associated with these inquiry pursuits. For example, a team may consider the actual consequences of failing to intervene in preventing early learning failure.

Step three in the process is incredibly important. Far too many teams have thoughtful conversations, get excited about a new direction, and then don't follow through with any meaningful action. If this protocol is used with a small group with relatively modest inquiry pursuits, action steps can be defined immediately and put into action. If it's applied in the context of a larger strategic planning session, the identification of work teams, priorities, and so on may lengthen the process. However, it's essential, once the question is engaged, that the group dedicate itself to immediately identifying the steps they'll take to pursue the answers. In order to improve organizational learning, teams need to feel confident that after they ask a thoughtful and strategic question, action will follow.

Step Four: Defining Accountability

Accountability is absolutely essential to making progress, not only from a systemic but also a psychological standpoint, as it builds an expectation for action and emotional engagement (Kuh, 2007). Use the following formative questions to build accountability into the normal working of the group:

- "What steps are we going to take as a group to evaluate our commitment to our questions and our progress in pursuing the answers to them? Will they become agenda items in our ongoing meetings? Will we establish a different type of follow-up protocol?"

- "Which individuals from within the organization do we need to engage in the pursuit of these inquiry statements? How connected do they need to be to our progress? What specific supports do we need from them in order to be successful?"

- "What supports do we require from outside the organization to give us momentum in moving forward? Are community, district, state, national, or international supports available?"

- "What additional steps can we take to hold ourselves and this process accountable? How can we ensure that this pursuit doesn't just disappear in our day-to-day grind?"

- "Are there other activities or objectives we could eliminate to create more time and mental focus for this pursuit? What objectives, activities, or priorities will we need to leave behind in order to make significant progress in this area?"

The question of outside help is particularly difficult for a number of reasons. First, because of our proclivity for isolation, we tend to shy away from asking for help (Rogers & Babinski, 2002). Once they reach out, schools are invariably shocked at the degree to which local, district, community, state, and national and international support systems are actually eager to give them support (Borja, 2005; Ocasio, 2005; Young, 2009). The final question is also challenging, because pre-K–12 education is notoriously ineffective in retiring goals and objectives that have outlived their usefulness (Campbell, 2003). They tend to go away by simply ignoring them long enough (Adelman & Taylor, 2007). At some point, you feel comfortable deleting that folder on your desktop that hasn't been opened for two years. This passive approach to change doesn't stimulate learning, confidence, or the commitment to learning and growth. However, being willing to give up some old priorities in the face of the identification of new ones builds in additional levels of accountability and creates momentum.

Step Five: Making the Agenda Public

It is also helpful to make the inquiry agenda known to the internal and external public in hopes that unexpected support will emerge. Most schools have experts in the community or benefactors waiting to engage once they recognize the need and are aware of the goals and objectives. This is why teams that are adroit at leveraging support let the public know what they're after. This commitment also creates a deeper sense of accountability, drive, and focus, because when a group or team goes public with a plan to drive change, it's much more difficult to simply ignore that objective in the months moving forward. For this step in the process, consider the following questions:

- "How can we make others aware of the pursuit of our questions?"

- "What new and innovative approaches can we take to bring our inquiry pursuits to individuals in our community and beyond?"

Step Six: Maintaining Engagement

Many times, groups become emotionally engaged in the short run and then find themselves bored, distracted, or overwhelmed. They then wind up taking relatively few steps toward the pursuit of their goals. The steps we articulated earlier will help, but it is even more important to keep the team emotionally engaged. The team has identified the rationale and the emotions connected with their inquiry pursuits, but in order to be effective, they must now revisit them on a consistent basis to keep them alive. As in personal relationships, focusing only on pedestrian tasks from day to day and forgetting about the deeper emotional commitment has its perils.

A series of meetings designed to examine policy or procedure related to change can be boring and arduous, but it will be less so if people are aware of the core questions the school staff is continually asking and answering, the emotional origins of those questions, and the outcomes they hope to stimulate.

Teams that are successful at executing this point in the process build in time to revisit their questions and reevaluate their level of emotional engagement. This can be done quarterly, monthly, or even more often if the pursuits are particularly difficult.

By applying this process of purpose-driven inquiry, teams become aware of the power of questions to shape a school improvement agenda. Furthermore, by establishing a system of asking and answering questions, it's likely that many more necessary questions will be generated. Inquiry pursuits can lead to elevated levels of confidence and curiosity and the eventual pursuit of more significant challenges. The development of relentless curiosity will also create a culture of fun, experimentation, and innovation. This progression is at the heart of organizational growth and change.

There is one caution teams need to observe, however: as their excitement and momentum build, they should try to avoid asking *too many* questions. Although schools tend to expand their capacity to manage a large and difficult inquiry agenda over time, from a growth standpoint, it's better to respond comprehensively to a smaller number of questions and see them through to fruition before overwhelming the process with many all at once. The number of questions a team can pursue effectively will be driven by the complexities of the challenge, the scope of the work, and most importantly, the limits of their imagination.

CHAPTER 6

Using Memory Systems to Stimulate Deep Organizational Learning

We used to believe that memory was a rather static, single-function mechanism that allowed us to keep a perfect record of our human experiences, like a camera that digitally encodes a scene. In recent years, we have learned that our system of making memories is much more fluid (Cohen & Conway, 2008). We know today that our memories are much less precise than we previously imagined, that a number of variables go into making and keeping memories, and that individual differences also shape this process. We have also learned recently that memory is not static—*how* we manage our ability to recall memory has an impact on *what* we remember. Finally, we've learned that the process of making, maintaining, and recalling memories is closely aligned to the learning process (Gathercole, Alloway, Willis, & Adams, 2006).

By having a better understanding of the conditions under which we best embed, maintain, rehearse, and recall memories, we can leverage our energies against a landscape of increased noise and distraction and bring old learning to bear on our newest challenges. A more thoughtful level of awareness about memory can have a significant impact on individual and team learning in schools.

Core Knowledge: Memory

We begin by exploring our core knowledge about the process of recording, rehearsing, and recalling memory.

Learning, Memory, and the Human Experience

All memories are not created equal. We may invest a great deal of time in an activity or experience—for example, driving hours on end through the desert—but devote very little mental or emotional energy to the experience, and as a result, we will have very little recollection of our time on the road. Conversely, we can have very brief but extremely significant experiences that we capture and neurologically encode as memory (Billington & Baron-Cohen, 2007). This process is often referred to as *firing and wiring* (Amitai & Connors, 1995). The neurons in the brain are engaged in direct proportion to our level of focus or emotional interest (Caine, Caine, McClintic, & Klimek, 2005; Bergan, Ro, Ro, & Knudsen, 2005). The greater the level of neuron stimulation, the more likely we are to capture the essence of a new learning experience and to ultimately make connections with other learning, formative events, abstract concepts, and related concrete experiences we have encoded earlier—or will encode later (Dillon, Ritchey, Johnson, & LaBar, 2007; Immordino-Yang & Damasio, 2007).

The *wiring* part of the firing and wiring equation refers to our capacity to connect this new learning with what we already know. After the brain "fires," the neurons snap to attention and the experience is "wired"—that is, it is encoded and compared against other memories and data points (VanRullen, Guyonneau, & Thorpe, 2005; Zheng & Tonnelier, 2008). The information is then classified in the brain over time—this is the process by which we make meaning of our experiences. An experienced teacher may attend a training session and quickly wire in the new knowledge she receives, thanks to all the old knowledge she had as a starting point. The more experience she has had, the easier it is to wire in the memories of the new event. We cannot, however, program into the brain *how* new information is wired or mentally categorized (Battro, Fischer, & Lena, 2008). How many times have you heard people reflect on their love or disdain for a particular academic area or discipline based on one teacher who made the experience either delicious or deplorable? Twenty years later, that memory is still wired in the same way, and new experiences are enjoyed or resisted based upon it.

Experiences that are relatively novel or abstract are more difficult to wire, because we don't have the previous associations (Fenker &

Schutze, 2008). For example, learning languages with words that have no direct translation in one's native language can be very difficult, particularly as we get older (Kersten & Earles, 2001); and if new learning is never appropriately wired, it will be difficult to fire those neurons again later and apply that learning in a new context.

We've always had a sense that the more dramatic the change efforts in school, the more thoughtful we need to be in our approach and the more patient we need to be through the implementation process. The notion of firing and wiring helps us to understand why this is the case.

What Is Recalled?

Our memories do not live within our heads like digitized copies of our favorite television shows. In fact, recent research has shown us that our memory systems are actually quite imprecise (Guerard & Tremblay, 2008; Friedman, 2007). Despite the amazing dexterity of the brain, we don't have the mental capacity or bandwidth to capture all the information around us (Belleville, Rouleau, Van der Linden, & Collette, 2003; Williams et al., 2006; Williams et al., 2007). Even memories that are particularly intense and emotionally bound are often void of many details and upon recall may be profoundly inaccurate. This is because the brain seeks out the most significant aspects of our experiences as they happen and captures details about their relevant components (Bergan, Ro, Ro, & Knudsen, 2005). In most cases, if you don't capture the details the first time, they won't suddenly become available later—leaving you with an incomplete recollection of the event (Foley, Foley, Scheye, & Bonacci, 2007; Marsh, 2007).

An Imperfect Act of Reconstruction

Since we tend to wire in our memories based on context and experience, the act of remembering is actually more an act of reconstruction than recall. Whatever we didn't capture or encode in the brain at the point of exposure of the event is subsequently "filled in" with what we think happened or how we imagine the event probably unfolded (Koenig & Mecklinger, 2008). This is why every year, in the story about the one that got away, the fish gets bigger.

This is also why members of a group recall the same event with so many divergent interpretations. They aren't being dishonest; their different life experiences have affected how they "saw" the events unfold, and their unique backgrounds change how the memory is reconstructed.

The Connection to Survival

Our natural systems for making memories have been crucial to our survival as a species. Recalling an escape from an alligator with large teeth was helpful at the sight of a tiger whose teeth were even larger! Even if we had never seen a tiger, our memory of any animal with large, dangerous-looking teeth would have been an asset. The capacity to recall discreet aspects of our experience allows us to benefit from our experiences more quickly. This is why experience is such a great teacher.

Reflection and Rehearsal

We reflect on memories that are important to us because reflection on and rehearsal (or reconstruction) of our memories makes them stronger. Even meaningful and emotionally relevant experiences will not be sustained in our brains very long unless we immediately begin to reflect on and evaluate them against previous knowledge, anticipated outcomes, and predicted application of these concepts (Egorov, Unsicker, & von Bohlen, 2006). This is also why you may think about something that happened to you and respond differently to it a day or two later. Through the reflection and rehearsal process, a memory also gets stronger, and as we create deeper and more comprehensive associations, a new memory is more easily retrieved (Miyashita, 2004; Tronson & Taylor, 2007). The best staff development sessions include time to reflect on the learning and perhaps practice a new skill, which creates a greater likelihood that deep learning will occur in the long run.

Typically, we don't pay enough attention to the power of reflection and rehearsal in relationship to organizational learning in schools.

Short-Term Memory and Working Memory

We used to believe that if we were able to capture information in our short-term memory and hold it long enough, it would eventually become part of our long-term memory. However, we have since discovered that the process isn't quite that simple. Most of the information that we detect through our senses is discarded immediately (Freeman, 2004). Some information, such as feelings of discomfort regarding the way we are sitting, for example, or a rise and fall in temperature, may result in subtle adjustments to our body's position or metabolism without distracting our focus (Jennings & van der Molen, 2005; Greenly, 1997). Most input, then, is handled subconsciously and immediately discarded due to its irrelevance (Davidoff, 2000). Your brain isn't tracking the adjustment you made to your posture in a meeting eleven years ago on the fifth of May.

If information does require analysis or evaluation, it is moved to the process within the brain commonly referred to as short-term memory (Nairne, 2002). There we begin to evaluate it against what we already know and what we anticipate will happen, and we rehearse aspects of the experience to ensure the maintenance of enough detail to recall the memory further if needed (Lee, Ee, & Ng, 2009; Tiede & Leboe, 2009).

Rather than transitioning this information to what we used to refer to as long-term memory, neurologists now believe we use a process called "working memory," an extension of our short-term memory that stores and evaluates information for future consideration but doesn't necessarily encode it in our minds forever. The relative durability of this information is driven by ongoing opportunities for recall, by its relevance, and by the emotional connections we associate with it (Gathercole, Alloway, Willis, & Adams, 2006).

In high school, we may have had a number of memorable experiences that were incredibly important that we used to negotiate our journey through adolescence. Twenty, thirty, or forty years later, we will not necessarily have forgotten what at the time was such an active component of our working memory, but we will not feel the emotional connections as much, due to their lack of relevance to our lives. The vividness of the information is likely to fade over time, as well. Looking back, we sometimes think that our memories are getting soft and we are forgetting. In reality, some of our memories have simply outlived their usefulness (Tronson & Taylor, 2007).

Solutions in Action: Memory and Deep Organizational Learning

This section offers a five-step protocol for promoting deep organizational learning based on what we know about memory. To illustrate, we use the example of a middle school called Gateway that is preparing to meet the rigorous demands of a new strategic planning process.

Step One: Establishing Intention

As we discussed in the previous section, for deep learning to occur, it is important to prepare those involved by giving them clues about what they can anticipate. In this way, learners can prepare themselves to recall aspects of their own experiences that might relate to this new learning. To assist in this process, ask the group to consider the following question: "What deep learning experiences am I hoping for as a result of this process?" When a team can collectively construct its intention, it begins to stimulate that part of the brain that specifically primes the memory system for learning.

Step Two: Applying Priming Strategies

After a clear vision of what is to be accomplished has been established, the next step is to begin to specifically "prime" the learning capacity of the team. To facilitate this process, the leadership team at Gateway Middle School asked themselves the following questions:

- "What steps can we take to prepare ourselves for this learning experience in order to make it authentic and durable?"

- "What types of emotions will we need to summon in order to make this learning journey successful?"

- "How can we formulate this journey into a specific and focused inquiry pursuit?"

In advance of a training, the Gateway Middle School leadership team made available articles and books related to the specific school-improvement strategy they were adopting. They also took time during faculty and departmental meetings to go over preliminary information regarding the upcoming training. This helped prime the collective intellect of the staff so they could take their learning experiences directly into their working memory for immediate and ongoing analysis and application.

The staff also talked about courage, pride, and determination—emotions they thought were necessary to make this comprehensive change possible. To forge a more direct connection with these emotions, they discussed specific students they hoped to affect and the community they wanted to serve and support.

In considering the last question, the team established a set of essential inquiry statements that were focused, strategic, and emotionally bound. When the day of the training finally arrived, team members were well read, emotionally primed, and focused on the learning objectives at hand, thanks to the inquiry pursuits they had identified.

Step Three: Firing the Neurons

In order to make deep learning possible, the brain needs to be stimulated. When our neurons are firing, we are active, alert, and ready to wire new experience into our memory system. To be strategic about the firing and initial wiring process, the Gateway staff asked the following question: "What can we do during the training to stimulate our individual and collective learning?"

The staff created collaborative work teams who would experience the training together—they knew that collaboration was much more likely to make their neurons fire at the highest levels (Chen & Kanfer, 2006). Furthermore, they decided that the firing and wiring process would be more engaging if the training included opportunities for immediate reflection and rehearsal, so the trainer built in time for team members to talk about what they had just learned and to apply strategies they had just been exposed to or discussed. By verbalizing, reflecting, and listening, levels of neurological engagement were once again increased.

The committee also built in learning breaks throughout the training. During these breaks, music, comic relief, food, and refreshments infused the learning experience with enjoyment and made it more emotionally engaging. By having fun and stimulating their endorphins, they were much more likely to remain engaged and encode a learning event more comprehensively.

Step Four: Wiring, Recalling, and Rehearsing

One of the biggest hindrances to deep learning is the lack of deep wiring opportunities. After an important event, we might spend a great deal of time recalling and discussing it as a means to process what we experienced. This leads to deeper and more durable mental representations. Even when events are meaningful and exciting, we don't necessarily recall them if we don't take time to reflect. In our example, the Gateway staff members decided that they would rededicate themselves to applying wiring, recall, and rehearsal strategies even after their training was over. To accomplish this task, the leadership team offered an optional, one-hour reflection session immediately following the training. This allowed interested learners to remain after the training and discuss the learning experience. The leadership team also put together a virtual learning space, which allowed people to post questions, share reflections, and begin to assemble resources. Digital natives and others who found this learning modality stimulating could then collaborate and wire in the learning in a deeper and more comprehensive manner.

The Gateway Middle School staff eventually built school-improvement reflection time into every meeting agenda that they could throughout the year. This included departmental, school improvement, and staff meetings. There was not always a great deal of time for reflection, but the simple inclusion of reflection on the agenda reinforced its importance.

It's important to keep in mind that during the wiring and reflection stage it is certainly okay if everyone doesn't agree. Schools historically are uncomfortable with philosophical disagreement, and some tend to see dissenting opinions as personal attacks, but thoughtful learning leaders must make it clear to teams that spirited intellectual discourse is extremely helpful. If done in a safe, fair, and productive context, it can create a more stimulating and rigorous learning environment. Debating ideas is much different than debating people: when debating ideas, it is perfectly fine to cross-examine the ideas themselves; it is not valuable to cross-examine others.

Rehearsal is another important aspect of organizational learning. If you were giving a major speech at a professional conference, you would very likely reflect on the content beforehand and mentally rehearse what you were going to say and how you were going to say it. Similarly, before applying a new teaching strategy, it is helpful to rehearse it. The bravest and most forward-thinking learning teams are willing to rehearse new learning with one another as a means for preparing for a future application. This might occur in a department meeting or in a classroom, with a teacher allowing fellow teachers to come in to observe, critique, and analyze his or her performance.

Many teams are not yet ready to embark upon this step. However, the willingness to rehearse creates an environment that rewards innovation, spurs experimentation, and facilitates deep learning processes.

Step Five: Evoking the Power of Celebration and Ceremony

Ceremony has always been extremely important in the transference of culture and tradition. Think about the importance a ceremony like graduation has to the mission and vision of a high school. Honoring retired teachers, formally welcoming new members to the staff, and supporting one another during the highs and lows in life's journey are also integral to the life of virtually every school. These ceremonies reinforce personal and professional priorities and enhance the emotional connections within the organization. Other schools may celebrate simply getting to the end of the year—a milestone that primarily puts the focus on escape, or have a tradition of "celebrating" new teachers by hazing them. These patterns send an altogether different message about the goals and priorities of the school.

At the end of the year, the learning team at Gateway decided to celebrate all the hard work they had done since embarking on their journey in deep learning. With the support of the parents' club, the leadership team threw a surprise party. Awards were given out for innovation, creativity, and even good humor. The team was careful to plan activities that were fun yet still in keeping with their goals, values, and beliefs. This end-of-year celebration became an annual event, and these awards were deeply valued within the organization.

Deep organizational learning cannot be left to chance or approached passively. Thoughtful learning leaders must develop a better understanding of how our natural memory systems work and what steps are needed to engage them more fully. When we consider the power of a motivated, focused, and thoughtful group of adults working together, time spent developing a more thoughtful approach to creating memories—and thereby nurturing deep learning—is well worth the investment.

CHAPTER 7

Handling Learning Overload

Schools today are teeming with talented, energetic, and well-intentioned teachers and administrators working every day at a fevered pitch. They come to school early, work hard all day, and stay late. At the end of the day, they may slump over in exhaustion as they think about the challenges that lie ahead. Interestingly, many schools exerting this degree of effort, when they look at their achievements at the end of the year, are shocked at just how little progress they make. Systemic problems and recalcitrant staff members derail progress at every opportunity. A dominant contributor to this overall lack of effectiveness is the feeling of learning overload. Learning overload can keep even well-intentioned high-energy leaders from making significant progress toward their most important goals. Learning organizations truly can't learn it all!

The problem of learning overload has grown as schools have become increasingly complex. Although technology was supposed to make our lives easier, most observers would probably agree that the massive influx of daily email and the monitoring that's required to keep up with all aspects of our virtual world have created more, not less, of a drain on our time and energy (Nworie & Haughton, 2008) and may actually diminish our mental energy (Sen, 2008).

We can't alter the brain to hold more information, but we can change our approach to learning in ways that reduce overwhelm and prepare us to deal with institutional challenges more effectively (Kennedy, 2006; Franklin, 2005).

Core Knowledge: Learning Overload

Let's look first at our core knowledge about the brain mechanisms that manage and organize large amounts of information.

Focal Points

The brain monitors a myriad of sensory inputs at any given time, but as we have pointed out, our attention is captured to a great extent by what we perceive as relevant (Kennedy, 2006). As our needs and interests evolve, our learning *focal points* shift, too, and the brain directs our attention in different directions. As adolescents, we may have been drawn to a television show related to sports or fashion. At middle age, our ears may perk up at a news report about the stock market or the emergence of a popular approach to child rearing. Neuroscientists refer to this mechanism in our brains as the *reticular activating system*. This mechanism serves to alert us when essential information is near (Izac, 2006)—that is, information that relates to one of the focal points we've established in our lives.

The most productive organizations are clear about their organizational focal points and don't ask their workers to focus on everything (Day, 2003; Roxborough, 2000; Tompkins, 2005). The most successful schools operate in the same way. One key to reducing stress and overwhelm is to clearly identify the learning focal points that matter.

The Cocktail Party Effect

If you are at a cocktail party and thirty different conversations are happening simultaneously, it's likely that you'll hear a wall of noise behind you as you participate in one of them. Suddenly, however, your head may tilt as you hear the name of your best friend mentioned ten feet away.

Psychologists and brain researchers refer to this as *the cocktail party effect* (Bronkhorst, 2000; Cherry, 1953). This mental capacity allows us to carry on with our normal lives and maintain a conscious level of focus on our life activities while subtly monitoring the environment for other relevant input. Obviously, the more we concentrate on the task at hand, the less likely we are to notice other influences going on around us (Brungart & Simpson, 2007).

Each of us clearly has only a set number of focal points we can focus on at any given moment (Barra, Bray, Sahni, Golding, & Gresty, 2005). Family, friends, and faith are three focal points that may change

very little throughout our lives. The focal points we continually monitor in our work depend on the choices we make and the values we collectively establish and support. Schools that are focused on harvesting
untapped potential look for strategies that will support those efforts.
Whether the issue is being whispered about at a cocktail party or for-
warded in an email, a school with a clear set of focal points is much
more likely to notice when something relevant comes along. Perhaps
this is the reason behind the old adage that lucky things happen to
hard-working people who are looking for the opportunity. If we are
focused on our goals, we turn our heads and listen when opportunities
whisper off in the distance.

Learning Capacity

Our individual learning capacities vary a great deal depending on
our age, genetics, and overall mental and physical health (Sorrell, 2008;
Kumar, Rakitin, Nambisan, Habeck, & Stern, 2008; Olsson et al., 2008;
Butterworth, 2005). Despite advances in brain research, we haven't
been able to come up with a mechanism to measure just how much
one person can know. We have learned, however, that learning capacity can be affected by factors such as priming and context and that it's
easy to get overwhelmed when we get too much information all at once
(Goldsborough, 2009; Sorrell, 2008).

Emotional relevance also influences learning capacity. A highly
motivated, deeply interconnected team with a passion for what they're
about to learn is more likely to recall and retain large amounts of new
learning than an unmotivated, disconnected, and disinterested working
group (Shu-Shen, 2008). It's clear that intellectual ability doesn't drive
learning capacity as much as connectedness, emotional relevance, and
context (Immordino-Yang & Damasio, 2007).

Chunking

Chunking is the strategy most of us use in remembering phone
numbers. We retain the area code (chunk one), the first three digits of
the phone number (chunk two), and the last four digits (chunk three).
Chunking is also referred to in relationship to our efforts to retain

large amounts of linear information, such as word lists (McElree, 2001; Oberauer, 2002; Cowan, Morey, & Chen, 2007).

In exercises with principals, I often provide a list of about fifty items that may typically appear on their "to do" lists. At first, the list seems overwhelming and confusing. Later in the training, I show the same items organized into categories, such as public relations, instruction and assessment, parent and community relations, and so on. There is an immediate sigh of relief, and the list, no longer so daunting, begins to make sense to the conference participants.

Learning leaders' individual and collective brains are always looking for emotional relevance and context to conceptualize and manage large amounts of information more effectively. By being aware of chunking, we can be much more thoughtful about organizing our work and conceptualizing the challenges we face.

Recall Codes

As we saw in the previous chapter, rehearsal and recall are important but not often discussed aspects of deep learning and memory. Efficient learners are able to systematically recall their experiences in a very focused and efficient way. Some of the brightest minds haven't necessarily stored information any more efficiently than other people but have simply developed more efficient recall strategies (Oberauer & Bialkova, 2009).

Individual and organizational learning can be dramatically affected by the degree to which we strategically apply recall strategies.

Solutions in Action: Organizational Focal Points

This section provides thoughtful learning leaders with an eight-step protocol that enables teams to work collaboratively to manage an overwhelming learning agenda. This protocol could provide the basis for conceptualizing a large school improvement initiative, or it could be used by smaller groups to organize their work and clarify their long-term efforts. It has been designed with an awareness of natural learning rhythms and the very real learning limits that affect us all.

Step One: Acknowledging Learning Limits

We are often under the mistaken impression that we can give genuine focus to several issues at once—that we can manage multiple priorities through some type of organizational multitasking. At any moment, however, each division of our attention, either individually or collectively, yields a diminished level of focus (Hayes & Freyd, 2002; Bayer, 2008; Gross, 2006).

In order to establish a more focused, effective, and less stressful work environment, collaborative teams must have honest conversations about learning limits. Simply put, teams need to acknowledge that *they can't learn it all.* In general, schools aren't good at setting these limits. We write grants for cutting-edge programs that require massive amounts of new learning. We adopt the latest curriculum and support materials that may or may not relate to the grant we just received. We resolve these issues by agreeing to add more to the learning agenda and then attempt to integrate math, writing, reading, multiculturalism, and technology across the curriculum. When a community challenge erupts, we agree to make time to learn the nuances of gang identifiers and lice detection. A good argument can be made that each of these issues is essential, and there may be a way to respond to most of these desires, but it's clear that the strategy of simply piling more onto an already overcrowded plate isn't the answer. Even though we may only be scratching the surface of what's possible for a productive learning organization, we can't expand our capacities without being thoughtful about the real learning limits that exist.

Identifying essential focal points is crucial to this process. Teams interested in expanding their capacities must therefore begin by limiting the careless expansion of organizational objectives. When new learning or action is introduced, the first question should be, "Does this expand our learning beyond our limits?" By consistently asking this question, we'll be in a better position to sort out those learning objectives that aren't necessary, while keeping that which is essential.

Obstructionists might read this and take it as confirmation that one more initiative will break the back of the organization. Teams must be strong at this point and acknowledge that in some cases, there already is too much to do, but in other areas, work may not be evenly distributed.

By acknowledging learning limits and establishing priorities, teams may find that ingenuity eventually allows them to do more.

Step Two: Lightening the Learning Load

Before a team has a thoughtful discussion about the learning focal points that are essential to its work, it can be helpful for team members to strategically evaluate goals that may have outlived their value to the organization—a process that this text refers to as *lightening the load*. It is important not to let this step impede your progress, since other steps in the protocol will also clarify focus and identify priorities and actions. However, when teams spend a few minutes identifying those objectives that may have become gratuitous, it's likely that they'll be more prepared to move forward in establishing defined learning focal points. To take this essential step in lightening the learning load, teams should ask themselves the following questions:

- "Are there any goals or objectives that we continue to talk about but have long abandoned?"

- "Do we know the difference between tasks and outcomes?"

- "Are we working more toward completing tasks or achieving outcomes?"

- "Do we all know the most important outcomes of our work?"

The first question attempts to honestly confront the tendency to support change initiatives that have already been abandoned by the group. Perhaps no one up to this point has been brave enough to recommend that the committee overseeing this initiative be disbanded or that the change effort be halted. Change efforts that are no longer being pursued often wind up being a burden on our time. People may be attending superfluous meetings, accomplishing irrelevant tasks, and taking care of unnecessary details just because no one has been willing to step forward and admit that it's time to move in another direction.

Some efforts just need to be set aside for a little while, not abandoned altogether. They may be good ideas, but other objectives have taken precedent for now. Every school has to make choices, and part of this process will be getting groups comfortable with the notion that the only way deep learning will occur and progress will improve is through our willingness to put aside items that are a lower priority.

The last three questions, relating to tasks and outcomes, are important because schools sometimes get bogged down with a laundry list of tasks that seem relevant but in reality have little relationship to an essential goal. In order to be effective, schools must sometimes ignore their tasks and refocus their efforts on their outcomes. Understanding the difference will be essential to moving forward.

Teams that are clear about outcomes are much more strategic about the tasks they choose to engage in. For example, most schools have identified as an outcome to strive for the establishment of a safe, orderly, and focused learning environment in which students respect themselves and each other. To meet that objective, some schools may have identified the management of the student dress code as a main component. The reformation of the dress code then takes on a life of its own. While some committees fervently study gang culture, others consider skirt length: getting the dress code right has taken the place of the actual intended outcome. This doesn't necessarily mean that a school should lighten the learning load by throwing out the dress code entirely, but they could for a year or more pull back from this focal point and leave some cognitive space for other objectives.

Step Three: Identifying Learning Focal Points

Ideally, a set of schoolwide learning focal points can give a much-needed sense of connection to the staff and lend symmetry to its work. In certain cases, the work of a subcommittee or small focus group may be complex enough to warrant a dedicated set of focal points related to its special goals or objectives.

The first step in establishing a focal point is to think about topics or issues that require consistent levels of attention. Tasks come and go, but focal points require long-term consideration. A school improvement team from New Zealand made up of teachers, curriculum specialists, and a principal created the following seven learning focal points:

1. Continuous learning and the collaboration process

2. Assessment and student achievement data

3.   Excellence in instructional practice

4.   Support materials, including textbooks and technology

5.   Partnerships and outside support

6.   Student support services and behavioral outcomes

7.   Innovation, emerging strategies, and new technology

Because the school improvement team that constructed this list didn't want to become overwhelmed, they chose only these seven areas to focus on, knowing full well that individually and collectively it's hard to manage much more than that. (This is also in keeping with what we learned about chunking.) It's also clear that this team was very thoughtful about the categories it chose and the wording used to shape each one. For example, the notions of continuous learning and collaboration processes relate back to the team's commitment to the power of working together and to the realization that growth is never-ending. The importance of focusing on student achievement data is obvious to most schools today, so the team naturally chose it as a focal point. The choice to recognize excellence in instructional practice reminded team members to continuously aspire to improve their instruction in order to stimulate learning.

Next, they deliberately referred to textbooks and technology as *support* materials, since they wanted to make sure the materials they chose did not dictate instruction. In the past, the school had been guilty of choosing materials that defined their work, and the team believed that thoughtful instructional beliefs should lead the way instead. The team also called out partnership as a focal point, because they realized that in the crush of their work each week this objective was almost always ignored. Rather than focusing on student discipline alone, they decided to regard student discipline and student support as one issue, which enabled them to keep the goal of supporting students in mind when dealing with the more controversial topic of discipline.

Finally, the group recognized that without innovation the organization would quickly fall behind. By specifically focusing on creative solutions, the team believed they could tap into the creative energies in their school that were waiting to emerge—an investment they felt would pay long-term dividends.

Step Four: Establishing Emotional Relevance

It is helpful, at this point, to identify the emotional relevance of each of the focal points that has been established. A simple way to assign emotional relevance is to ask the following questions:

- "Why is this focal point important to the group?"

- "Why does this focal point deserve our consistent attention?"

For example, the school improvement team felt that by building a learning community and supporting collaboration teachers could grow closer as colleagues and would share ideas and strategies. They also believed they would be working smarter as well as adding to the joy of everyone's work. Their desire to focus on sponsorships arose from the realization that there were so many talented and willing parents and community members who legitimately cared about the mission of the school, had been untapped for decades, and were waiting to serve. The desire to focus on emerging strategies and technology was spawned from the desire to overcome a long-standing fear within the group about change related to the application of technology. This group decided to turn what had been a fear and weakness into a focal point and strength.

Step Five: Establishing Inquiry

The next step is to identify an overarching question that captures the intent of this particular focal point pursuit. As indicated earlier, the brain tends to become more engaged when we see our challenges formulated as questions. Questions add specificity and accountability and they help us seek specific answers. Table 7.1 (page 108) shows the questions the school improvement team developed to go with each focal point.

Asking questions in a more empowering and focused manner isn't just a mental exercise. It provides meaningful clues that direct mental and emotional energies in pursuit of outcomes. In examining these inquiry statements, notice that they are broad and general. They are not designed to give teams a definitive action plan or prescriptive steps to follow. Instead, they are meant to keep us mentally and emotionally aimed in the right direction and focused on the right overarching priorities. We can't keep the nuance of every aspect of a complex strategic plan in our minds all the time. However, since questions drive our focus and can help to quickly and efficiently shape our emotional set points, asking the right questions in broad contextual terms can keep us moving in the right direction. Note that some inquiry statements can be both general and specific: "How can we cut the dropout rate in half in two years?" "How can we increase the number of students going on to college after they graduate?" The specificity of these questions may be derived from a more generalized sense of what needs to get accomplished.

Table 7.1: Questions for the Seven Focal Points

1.	Continuous learning and the collaboration process	Can collaboration lead to deep levels of innovation, improved performance, and a more fun and interesting work environment?
2.	Assessment and student achievement data	Will our new system of collaborative assessment improve student achievement and give us a greater sense of direction in establishing our instructional practices?
3.	Excellence in instructional practice	Can we come to an agreement as to what excellent instruction looks like in our school? How can we support it?
4.	Support materials, including textbooks and technology	Will our system of material adoption result in improved levels of student achievement and the strategic identification of the best resources available for our curriculum?
5.	Partnerships and outside support	Will our outreach programs engender deeper levels of support within the local community for our instructional program and instill deeper levels of understanding regarding our mission, goals, and values?
6.	Student support services and behavioral outcomes	Will our new system of managing student behavior create a more dignified and learning-centered approach in supporting students?
7.	Innovation, emerging strategies, and new technology	Will the application of our new technology training program rejuvenate a technology-wary staff, better connect with our technology-savvy students, and ultimately result in higher levels of student achievement?

In examining the inquiry statements in table 7.1, it is clear that the authors have an expanded vision for what they hope to achieve. For example, when looking at question three, "Can we come to an agreement as to what excellent instruction looks like in our school? How can we support it?" rather than simply examining evaluations at the end of the year, the team sought to pursue a deeper set of objectives and to approach the problem with a broader scope. For question six, rather than having a discipline committee, evaluating the demerit schedule, or focusing on punishment options, this school improvement team once again focused on outcomes and put the emphasis more broadly on student support and behavior. This broader context helped minimize the distractions.

Step Six: Identifying Essential Goals and Outcomes

For this step in the process, the team got specific about goals or outcomes that make a difference. Team members were asked to identify one or two "nonnegotiable must-haves"—goals they will achieve no matter what by the end of the year in relationship to each of the focal points they established (table 7.2 , page 110). These outcomes are essentially promises a school makes to itself that, if all else fails, they *will* bring these important outcomes to fruition. It is helpful for teams who do this to select goals that are somewhat impervious to the ebb and flow of district funding and largely within the control of the staff members involved, rather than, for example, ones that could fall apart with a budget crisis. Neither should teams make their indispensable goals the most expensive or complex ones on the list. This will allow the team to make progress toward their outcome in an otherwise challenging year.

Imagine how proud teams would be if at the end of the year, they had met or exceeded a quarter or even half of their goals. Some teams will be forward-thinking enough to achieve them all. However, in this step of the process, it is best not to overplan but to simply identify goals that should come before anything else.

Table 7.2: Nonnegotiable Must-Have List

1. Continuous Learning and the Collaboration Process	
Goal 1: Give all staff members training in the learning community process by November of this school year so that they can participate on a learning community team in regularly scheduled meetings after the November training session until the end of the year.	Goal 2: As a companion to the learning community implementation process, launch a virtual learning space that will allow dialogue to continue in a synchronous fashion and enable continuous learning, growth, and improvement.

2. Assessment and Student Achievement Data	
Goal 1: Establish a comprehensive testing bank for agreed-upon essential learning units by grade level and subject area by the end of the year.	Goal 2: Gather meeting minutes regarding collaborative assessment discussions, and provide quarterly feedback on the collaborative assessment process.

3. Excellence in Instructional Practice	
Goal 1: Establish a research-based list of instructional best practices. This list will be shared with the rest of the teachers during the second semester in an attempt to develop a vision for what excellence in instruction means in the school.	Goal 2: After the completion of the excellence-in-instruction practice document, recognize teachers who demonstrate these practices with a brief description of their lessons in monthly faculty meetings.

4. Support Materials, Including Textbooks and Technology	
Goal 1: By the end of the first semester, all of the books, hardware, software, and related web links and services that are required to teach each course will be identified.	Goal 2: By the end of the first semester, the school's curriculum development team will apply a force-field-analysis strategy in which textbooks and other materials will be adopted for use in the classroom based on the direct correlation between the material and the district's rated course of study for each class.

5. Partnerships and Outside Support	
Goal 1: The Partnerships Committee will identify three additional community benefactors to support the field trip and student assembly fund for the following year.	Goal 2: A plan will be developed and implemented for a community open house in the spring, showcasing the school's outstanding academic achievements and the connections that are being made to business and industry.

6. Student Support Services and Behavioral Outcomes	
Goal 1: Offer an optional study group on *Creating Classrooms Where Teachers Love to Teach and Students Love to Learn,* by Robert Sornson (2005), and seek CEU credits for staff participation.	Goal 2: Schedule a *Creating Classrooms Where Teachers Love to Teach and Students Love to Learn* training session in the spring to implement the love and logic approach to student behavior for the following year.

7. Innovation, Emerging Strategies, and New Technology	
Goal 1: Establish a venture capital fund financed by at least three grants of $500 each for local research and development.	Goal 2: Establish a technology-innovators team of staff members who consistently lead the way in technology breakthroughs, and provide at least twenty minutes in a faculty meeting quarterly for them to demonstrate their latest innovations to the entire staff.

Step Seven: Making the Focal Points Public

The next important step in the focal point process is to make the overarching questions and goals available to all members of the staff as well as to interested individuals in the general public. When community members are aware of what a school is trying to accomplish, they will often come forward with unexpected resources. Furthermore, in far too many schools some teachers are passionately pursuing an important outcome while their colleagues working next door are completely unaware of their pursuits. If your neighbors don't know, they can't lend a hand. A big part of driving deeper levels of learning and change is having the courage to step up and be clear about what you are after and the kind of growth you seek.

If you are not willing to talk about your dreams, goals, and learning objectives in your own school, you are not likely to make significant progress. This is another area where courage pays dividends.

Step Eight: Funneling New Ideas Into Current Focal Points

The learning focal point process can also be used to limit the learning agenda if necessary. Schools are much more likely to make progress when new issues come up each year if schools can limit issues to those related to their focal points. A school staff will feel more comfortable engaging an issue for which it already has a context. For example, if a parent group decides it wants to help, the school improvement team may have a focal point that relates to partnership. If Apple Corporation decides to launch a test-site classroom, teachers on the school improvement team who have a focal point regarding emergent strategies and new technology will know where that new influence should be mentally and emotionally filed.

The identification of learning focal points, empowering questions, and must-have outcomes won't reduce all the confusion in an organization. However, it will go a long way toward establishing which priority items will truly make a difference in improving student learning. Where there is a sense of clarity about goals and objectives, there also tends to be a deeper sense of calm and security about the future of the organization.

CHAPTER 8

Creating a Defined Learning Culture

Learning is dramatically affected by a number of environmental factors that are within our control (Campbell & Bigger, 2008; Tapola & Niemivirta, 2008; Merritt, 2008). While studying in school, you may have found a special place where doing your homework or studying for a test was easy. When the stakes were high and the desire was great, you took yourself to this tried and true learning spot, believing that it somehow improved your capacity to take learning to a deeper level. Given our intuitive sense for putting ourselves in environments that support learning, wouldn't it be ideal if we intentionally established learning environments that supported individual and collaborative adult learning at the highest levels?

If a learning culture does not have a thoughtful strategy of its own, variables like fear, isolation, and distraction can easily become definitive forces. Because we know so much more today about what it takes to create a learning environment that supports deeper levels of cognition, learning leaders can purposefully create what we refer to as a *defined learning culture,* an environment that maximizes our capacity to learn.

Core Knowledge: Defined Learning Cultures

In this section, we will explore the foundational elements related to creating a defined learning culture. These core elements will help leaders visualize the steps they can take to shape this journey.

Competing Mental Representations and Deep Learning

An essential aspect of knowledge acquisition is the comparison of new information with old. When we experience something new, we compare and contrast it to what we already know (Scott & Dienes, 2008). In fact, trying to comprehend foreign concepts without any previous mental representations with which to compare them represents our most difficult learning challenge (Brehmer et al., 2008). Similarly, it is very difficult to learn something if the new data compete with or somehow contradict a previously held belief or knowledge point (Kimmerle, Moskaliuk, & Cress, 2008; Dochy, Segers, & Buehl, 1999).

Suppose a middle school civics teacher provided her class with a series of interesting learning experiences revolving around equity, fairness, and civil rights. A child from a family that has always taught him a sense of fairness and respect for fellow human beings might grasp the learning experience with enthusiasm and familiarity. In this case, the new learning coincides with mental representations that he already possesses, thanks to parental influence. The civics lesson would reinforce previous learning and create an even more durable mental representation.

Conversely, if a child is growing up in an intolerant, racist environment where the antithesis of these life lessons has been promulgated from day one, the civics teacher's lessons would create a sense of doubt and confusion. The child's ability to accept the new learning and create a durable mental representation would be hindered by the fact that the new knowledge was in direct conflict with the old. Competing mental representations influence deep learning.

Relaxed Alertness

Many learning theorists in recent years have come to the conclusion that the most preferred emotional state for deep learning is *relaxed alertness*, a state in which we are relaxed yet emotionally engaged when facing new learning challenges (Caine, Caine, McClintic, & Klimek, 2005). This makes a great deal of sense. In an emergency, panic or fear might drive our ability to learn a new skill at a high rate of speed—out of the simple but essential desire to continue our time on earth! Despite the increased level of engagement, fear tends to shift the brain into fight or flight, a mental state that keeps the mind racing but doesn't necessarily promote the deepest levels of reflection (Davies & Osguthorpe, 2003). If we are overexcited, we are less reflective about what we are experiencing and how that information relates to previous learning (Ward, 2008). On the other hand, when we are too relaxed, we don't experience the stimulation, focus, and energy that thrust us forward and accelerate learning levels (Goetz, Frenzel, Pekrun, Hall, & Ludtke, 2007; Pekrun, Goetz, Titz, & Perry, 2002). Even if the perfect level of relaxed alertness is difficult to find in practice, establishing it as a goal creates a more focused and defined learning culture.

Context

The simplicity of the concept of context belies its subtlety, which is why we will examine it from several key perspectives.

Situational Context

The *situational context* for learning refers to its physical location, timing, and any local cultural factors that might affect its durability (Thompson & Wheeler, 2008; Primary Review, 2008). Even a well-intentioned, focused, and high-performing school may not learn as effectively if it is holding a professional development training session the day before a major holiday or the day after the death of a beloved colleague. Conversely, a school that learns it has finally received a major grant might approach a learning situation with a renewed sense of enthusiasm and focus. Controlling and shaping those situational factors that are within our control helps improve learning (Brehmer et al., 2008).

Interpersonal Context

Interpersonal context refers to the impact on learning of variables related to an individual's personal life circumstances. These include such factors as ascribed status within a group, gender, ethnicity, economic standing, beliefs, performance expectations, and attitudes toward school, learning, and previous learning experiences (Arievitch & Haenen, 2005; Hickey & Zuiker, 2005; Stone & Lane, 2003; Abedi & Gandara, 2006). If a number of teachers on a staff were expectant mothers or fathers or were dealing with dying parents or impending divorces, these life-changing events would affect their individual and collective focus and attention. The decision to go back to graduate school represents an example of an interpersonal context that could enhance learning.

Physical Context

Physical context relates to the conditions in which learning takes place (Merritt, 2008). These can include temperature, light, the relative comfort of the room, access to fresh air, acoustics, and other factors that affect people's sensory experiences. Our brains are sufficiently different that some people may find their learning accelerates in a cool room, while others may feel distracted by the lower temperature. Some brains prefer dim light; others need access to natural, direct light in order to promote high levels of mental alertness (Jacobs, 2003). If our environment is comfortable but not stimulating, it's likely to promote deep sleep instead of deep learning. The best physical context is comfortable, stimulating, yet free of distraction.

Another example of physical context relates to the associations we have with a particular learning space (Rydeen & Erickson, 2002; Graetz & Goliber, 2002). The power of physical context has caused many school administrators to reconsider giving high-stakes tests in locations like gymnasiums and cafeterias. Some recommend studying for a test in the same lecture hall where the test will be given. Familiarity of physical context assists in establishing a strong learning environment.

Consolidation

Consolidation refers to the time we take to reflect on our experiences en route to deep learning (Lupien & Schramek, 2006). Learning takes time to gel. When we experience a meaningful event, we may spend hours, days, months, or even years grappling with the information and considering how it relates to what we already know. This process of digging back into our memory, recalling old learning opportunities, and evaluating them against our new learning experiences allows us to create new connections and identify unique disconnects that we may need to resolve (Strong-Wilson, 2006; Lee & Birdsong Sabatino, 1998).

The power of consolidation may cause you to awaken in the middle of the night or first thing in the morning with a number of ideas about things you had been thinking of the previous day. While we sleep, the brain is free from the burden of processing our every move, and during that time your gray matter goes into search mode, reflecting back on issues or ideas you've been considering in hopes of learning something new and applying it later when needed (Peters, Ray, Smith, & Smith, 2008; Seung-Schik, Hu, Gujar, Jolesz, & Walker, 2007). When your mother said to sleep on it, you should have listened!

When we allow the brain the time it needs, we are likely to arrive at much more profound levels of application (Cohen & Robertson, 2007). In certain extremely intense learning environments, learners are expected to respond to copious amounts of new learning over an extended period of time. In these environments, they are likely to forget a great deal of what they've been exposed to because they are expected to begin learning new information before they have had an opportunity to reflect on what they've experienced. These stressful, overburdened environments can result in diminished learning and a decreased capacity to manage the deepest levels of application (LaBar, 2007; Cahill, Prins, Weber, & McGaugh, 1994).

Enemies of a Defined Learning Culture

In order to create a defined learning culture, we must be aware of factors, like the following, that can distract us from this outcome:

- **Deadlines**—Deadlines may create a sense of focus, but if they are constantly too short, the opportunity to allow learning to consolidate is lost. Thus, the most creative solutions may never be discovered.

- **Disorganization**—Learning is diminished by disorganization (Awartani, Whitman, & Gordon, 2008; Upitis, 2004). While it's clear that each of us may have different levels of tolerance, a constantly disorganized environment hinders our progress.

- **Illogical expectations**—Schools that say yes to every change may find themselves with a completely illogical set of change and growth expectations. This leads to deep levels of distraction, stress, and a diminished learning environment.

- **Exhaustion**—Some schools have been exposed to year after year of incomplete and disconnected change initiatives. This lack of coherence can leave staffs feeling overwhelmed and exhausted—feelings that diminish the learning environment.

- **Lethargy**—Relaxed alertness is ignited by passion and commitment. If staff members are generally passive and lethargic, they may feel relaxed but won't be alert enough to push themselves to the next level of learning, growth, and change.

Solutions in Action: Establishing a Defined Learning Culture

In this section, we introduce a six-step process that will help learning leaders create a high-functioning, defined learning culture.

Step One: Make Relaxed Alertness a Goal

In pursuit of the right emotional tenor, relaxed alertness should be a nonnegotiable. The team in charge of planning professional development could examine what types of activities to include throughout its training sessions that could keep the staff excited and engaged while enjoying a sense of comfort and safety. Principals can do the same when planning a faculty meeting.

A number of strategies suggested in this book can be helpful in promoting relaxed alertness. The change, analysis, and reframing strategy (page 33) helps keep the fear of change in check. Our work on reducing stress factors (chapter 3), clarifying our mental images or vision (chapter 4), establishing more focused and empowering questions (chapter 5), and minimizing learning overload (chapter 7) can all help to make learning clearer and less overwhelming, again promoting the state of relaxed alertness.

Step Two: Identify Competing Mental Representations

It's difficult to have a defined learning climate if competing mental representations create confusion. Learning leaders must constantly be on the lookout for competing mental representations and bring these conflicts to the forefront for discussion and analysis.

Table 8.1 offers a number of essential mental representations regarding leadership, change, teaching, learning, and students. These areas were chosen because they often create dichotomies that aren't always easy to resolve.

Table 8.1: Competing Mental Representations in Schools

Below each set of competing mental statements is a Likert scale. Identify to what degree you are committed to one representation or another, with - 5 being the least and + 5 being the greatest degree of identification. A score of 0 means that you see both perspectives equally.

The genesis of change in our school: the principal's office or the classroom?

Schools can't change until something significant happens in the principal's office.

vs.

True change happens when new actions are taken in the classroom.

Principal's office 5—4—3—2—1—0—1—2—3—4—5 Classroom

Leadership: a position or a capacity to influence?

In our school, people become leaders once they are given a job title.

vs.

Leadership is the capacity to influence the environment, allowing staff with talent and vision to step up when they are ready.

By position 5—4—3—2—1—0—1—2—3—4—5 Capacity to influence

Fear: use it or keep it at bay?

We make progress by using fear to keep people in line.

vs.

We make progress by diminishing fear in the culture.

Using fear 5—4—3—2—1—0—1—2—3—4—5 Keeping it at bay

The leader's role: safe stalwart or risk taker?

We lead by example by always playing it safe.

vs.

We lead by example by taking bold but calculated risks in the name of change.

Safe stalwart 5—4—3—2—1—0—1—2—3—4—5 Risk taker

The leader's role: master or servant?

We get the most out of others by giving them very clear direction and constant supervision.

vs.

We get the most out of others by identifying their needs and supporting their growth.

Master 5—4—3—2—1—0—1—2—3—4—5 Servant

---

continued on next page→

The leader's role: finding faults or finding strengths?

Our job is to find faults in others and correct or replace them.

vs.

Our job is to adroitly find strengths in others and nurture them.

Faults 5—4—3—2—1—0—1—2—3—4—5 Strengths

Change: episodic or continuous?

We expect change in our school to come in fits and starts.

vs.

We know that change is the only thing that's constant.

Episodic 5—4—3—2—1—0—1—2—3—4—5 Continuous

Collaboration: cheating or learning?

Teachers and administrators work in relative isolation, and collaboration is almost analogous to cheating.

vs.

Collaboration is a corporate expectation and is seen as the key to learning.

Cheating 5—4—3—2—1—0—1—2—3—4—5 Learning

Change solutions: prepackaged or cocreated?

Leaders decide on a change plan and then systematically implement it, attempting to secure buy-in.

vs.

Change plans are cocreated, relying on the vision, goals, and aspirations of everyone involved..

Prepackaged 5—4—3—2—1—0—1—2—3—4—5 Cocreated

The purpose of school: reflect and maintain community standards or advance them?

Leaders (including teacher leaders) continue to construct a school in the image of the community, reflecting current standards and beliefs.

vs.

Leaders (including teacher leaders) create a school designed to advance community standards and support purposeful community improvement and renewal.

Reflect 5—4—3—2—1—0—1—2—3—4—5 Advance

Teaching: teaching curriculum or teaching students?

Leaders (including teacher leaders) work to ensure the content is taught.

vs.

Leaders (including teacher leaders) work to make sure the students learn.

Curriculum 5—4—3—2—1—0—1—2—3—4—5 Students

Assessment: catching and sorting or identifying and intervening?

Assessment is used to catch students who are lazy
or unprepared en route to sorting them out.

vs.

Assessment is used to identify learning challenges and establish a plan for intervention.

Catch and sort 5—4—3—2—1—0—1—2—3—4—5 Identify and intervene

Learning goals: teaching to standard or adding value?

Our role is to ensure that students reach a prescribed standard.

vs.

Our role is to recognize students' capacity and work toward systematically
adding value and helping the students realize growth and improvement.

Reaching Standard 5—4—3—2—1—0—1—2—3—4—5 Adding value

Student capacity: empty vessels or unharvested fields?

Students are empty vessels who come to school to be filled with knowledge.

vs.

Students come to school with unseen talent and skills, like fields waiting to be
harvested by teachers—and by the students themselves.

Vessels 5—4—3—2—1—0—1—2—3—4—5 Fields

Recalcitrant learners: rejected and ostracized or embraced and studied?

We reject struggling or recalcitrant learners due to their poor performance,
attitude, and inability to get along with others.

vs.

We carefully study recalcitrant learners and treat their behaviors
as symptoms leading to a treatment and a cure.

**Rejected and ostracized 5—4—3—2—1—0—1—2—3—4—5 Embraced and
studied**

continued on next page→

> **Snapshot of good teaching: teacher in motion vs. students in motion?**
>
> Teachers are seen as effective if they are very busy and active in their classrooms.
>
> vs.
>
> Teachers are seen as effective if the students are very busy and active in their classrooms.
>
> **Teacher in motion 5—4—3—2—1—0—1—2—3—4—5 Students in motion**

Visit **go.solution-tree.com/leadership** to download and print this resource.

Tabulating the Results

Clearly, there are no right or wrong answers in evaluating these mental representations. Most schools ebb and flow with each of these issues, depending on the leadership force and the social context, which is continually affected by new members coming into the organization. However, a forward-thinking learning organization using the themes consistently presented in this book will try to minimize competing mental representations and function with more of a collective mind. If half of the staff believes that change occurs only when the principal does something in his or her office, a push toward profound transformation in the classroom won't seem relevant. Leaders at all levels need to be risk takers, and the principal and prominent teacher leaders must work as servants, not masters. Schools that can move to the right on this scale for most of these issues will be implementing many of the key focal points presented in this book and will be in alignment with what we know about individual and collective learning.

Step Three: Prepare for Situational Contextual Influences

It's clear that we can't control every situation that might affect our organizational learning. However, some choices we make in relationship to organizational learning should be made with an eye to situational context. For example, when we plan, our learning means a lot. A staff that socializes every Friday afternoon after school may not be as tuned in to a meeting held at that time. The beginning and end of a school year bring a different situational context to any learning environment, as will the times around holidays like Thanksgiving. There are very real advantages from a learning standpoint to picking a time that minimizes distraction.

Learning leaders must remain aware of emotional outliers at the local, community, national, or international levels. A school that is on the verge of winning a state championship in football after generations of academic and athletic failure may be distracted and hopeful. Dramatic shifts in the community's economy may be affecting students, parents, and the teachers who work with them. A school with a number of staff and students from the Middle East might respond differently to an international event in that area, such as a war, than a school with few people who have cultural and familial connections to that area.

Step Four: Prepare for Interpersonal Contextual Influences

Learning leaders can't control the interpersonal challenges any of us might face. They can, however, attempt to create a working environment that's supportive, collaborative, and safe. On any staff there will be deaths, births, divorces, and weddings and any number of other events that can leave people feeling challenged or distracted. Some schools have committees devoted to maintaining levels of support when colleagues are in trouble. These teams might keep files with identified action steps for supporting colleagues in specific ways. This level of thoughtfulness and planning allows us to feel more emotionally associated with our place of work and ultimately reduces the distraction that results if any of these personal situations are handled poorly.

Step Five: Prepare for Physical Contextual Influences

Learning leaders must take basic precautions to make sure that the physical context of the environment is conducive to deep learning. Relatively simple changes can result in a more comfortable, focused, and relaxed atmosphere.

The temperature of the room, for example, must be relatively comfortable for all of the people there. The quality of the lighting is also essential. Natural light dramatically increases the amount of stimulation to the brain (Vandewalle et al., 2007). Working in a dark room can be frustrating when our learning expectations involve reading or activities where the darkness inhibits our capacity to process the information. The relative comfort of the seating is also essential; an uncomfortable desk can create stress and distraction.

Other issues that relate to physical context include hunger and thirst. As we have said earlier, relieving hunger and thirst can result in an endorphin release and more positive associations with whatever activity is going on at the time (Murphy, 2007). This is why eating is so closely associated with celebrations. The acoustics in the room also make a difference. The stress and frustration that arise if we can't hear one another well distract from the learning. A room that isn't properly ventilated can cause problems as well. A lack of oxygen can make the brain become concerned about survival rather than the deep learning at hand.

Another important physical contextual issue is the size of the room and its usual function. If a meeting is held where people feel crowded, cramped, or psychologically trapped, they won't be very reflective in their thinking. If a room typically has a physical context related to some application other than learning, it is likely to be a distraction. This is why cafeterias aren't great locations for test taking or staff development.

Step Six: Apply Consolidation Strategies

Consolidation, as we have seen, involves allowing time after initial exposure for learning to develop. The exact amount of time a leader should give to consolidation isn't an exact science. It is generally agreed that the more challenging the learning experience, the more time your brain will need to mull it over (Robertson, 2009). Taking time to reflect immediately after learning something new or going through a planning session is helpful, followed by an opportunity to revisit the learning soon thereafter—perhaps after several days. Consolidation is at work when, the day after a faculty meeting, the staff comes back with more thoughts about the previous day's discussion. Since this happens naturally, the best practice is to build this stage into the learning process whenever possible. The other advantage to building in consolidation is that it forces the staff to be less rushed—an outcome that reduces stress and fear overall.

To ensure that consolidation is taking place, a learning leader can take advantage of the three *R*s: repetition, rehearsal, and reflection. Repetition may seem like a somewhat pedestrian approach to deep learning, but hearing the same thing several times in different ways can help bring about deep learning, especially when you are struggling with a difficult challenge or idea. Rehearsal is a means for giving staff a chance to practice the new learning they've experienced. This might involve trying out a new teaching strategy in a department meeting or some other kind of practice situation that is relatively low risk and high in stimulation and reward. Finally, consolidation is built on the concept of reflection. Some staff members like to reflect alone, while others may choose to talk their ideas through with friends or colleagues. Either way, it is time well spent.

Asking questions without expecting answers right away is another step learning leaders can take to support consolidation. We have a tendency in our culture to seek solutions very quickly. However, there's nothing wrong with allowing some questions to go unanswered for a while. This strategy can stimulate deeper levels of engagement and make the consolidation process more engaging and rigorous.

The development of a defined learning culture is a commitment to a never-ending process. The learning environment will never be perfect for everyone. Factors will always arise that keep us from being at our level best at every minute, but dedication to this ongoing construction will pay a number of dividends. By being aware of the power of relaxed alertness and mental representation and by understanding the effect of disconnects, the influence of context, and the importance of consolidation, learning leaders can bring about change at the deepest levels.

Inspired Collaboration

Schools have become increasingly intrigued by collaboration. With the proliferation of learning communities, many schools are now using teams to overcome the effects of anachronistic styles of management and to help resolve their deepest school improvement challenges (DuFour, DuFour, & Eaker, 2008). Nevertheless, many schools that are attempting to collaborate in one form or another are making very little progress toward their goals.

It is ironic that collaboration is an issue in an era of instant messaging, Twitter, email, and asynchronous dialogue. However, while new technology creates opportunities to collaborate, other obstacles persist. The difference in perspectives between Net Generation individuals (those who grew up with digital technology) and pre–Net Generation individuals (those who "emigrated" to the digital technology) is one of the many challenges.

Regardless of the technological tools in use, from a learning leadership perspective collaboration has one essential outcome—to improve individual and team learning. The collaborative learning process should result in a change in attitudes, beliefs, skills, and strategies that affect the essential goal of the organization—instructional practice. With collaboration, learning is ignited—and many schools are very close to lighting that learning fire.

Core Knowledge: Collaboration

In the following section, we explore our core knowledge regarding collaboration by looking at the strengths it brings to the learning environment.

Collaboration Stimulates Individual and Group Learning

The durability of the mental representations that we create is driven by the amount of neurological stimulation devoted to an experience or a learning task (Ressler & Mayberg, 2007). Research has shown that in many instances collaboration stimulates our brain to a greater extent than working alone does (Achterman & Loertscher, 2008; Chapman, Ramondt, & Smiley, 2005). It therefore allows us to draw forth a greater degree of mental energy when attempting to learn something new. Collaborative learning has a symbiotic relationship with individual learning: the brain, in categorizing new learning and evaluating the mental associations we bring to our experiences, relies on context clues from those around us to help us assemble these categories. Thus, our ability to reflect in isolation is shaped by the experiences we have in collaboration (Merrill & Gilbert, 2008).

Collaboration Challenges Inconsistencies and Enhances Perspective

All of us have blind spots in our learning. Perspectives based on past experiences keep us from either making necessary associations or from evaluating what's put in front of us. To risk restating the obvious, one of the great values of teams in school is the diverse set of perspectives, cultures, and backgrounds they bring to new learning. If what we learn is driven to a great extent by our previous experiences and the associations we can make, then collaboration gets us as close as we will ever get to certain experiences without having lived someone else's life.

Collaboration Tests Values and Beliefs

Even if a school—or any other organization—consistently supports certain values and beliefs, it's easy to forget them if they aren't practiced. A school that believes all children can learn has that value tested when it has to decide what to do about students who are not meeting standard on a state test. In fact, team members may have multiple perspectives on what that value means and how it should be demonstrated. While there is likely to be disagreement, such discussions are invaluable, because they serve to define organizational values and beliefs and ultimately to shape behaviors in ways that reflect the collective hearts and minds of staff members.

A person who collaborates may come into the conversation with one perspective on an essential value or belief and leave with a completely different idea about what it actually means.

Collaboration Establishes Accountability

When groups collaborate constantly regarding important learning outcomes, the act of collaboration itself establishes a degree of accountability (Horwitz & Horwitz, 2007). While teachers or principals toiling in isolation may set high standards for themselves, the failure to meet those standards has few consequences absent some degree of public examination. Accountability works as a check on expectations as well: those who work in isolation may hold themselves to an unreasonable standard and it may take a collaborative effort to convince staff members to stop beating themselves up and start making progress.

Collaboration Builds Memories and Stimulates Emotional Ties

The science is clear that collaboration tends to elevate levels of emotion (Goleman & Boyatzis, 2008). When we feel good about something, we're likely to feel even better when we're with a group. If we're processing a difficult challenge, we'll feel more confident and courageous about it when other group members feel the same. Neurologically, we have a tendency to pull our emotional states into congruence, and that allows us to be more deeply connected to each other and the organization (Fadul, 2007). Therefore, schools that collaborate consistently have a more realistic chance of developing staff members who are mentally and emotionally committed to the organization and its outcomes.

Furthermore, since our memory systems are driven to a great extent by the emotions we have when creating a memory, it's clear that collaboration supports the process of reflecting and reconstructing our essential learning experiences. A team may get together and relive a victory several dozen times over a five-year period, and that reconstruction will help embed the memory of it in a deep and meaningful way—with a potentially profound long-term impact on the teams' belief in itself and its conceptualization of the future.

Collaboration Provides Rewards

In comparison to many other species, humans don't fare all that well alone. In fact, collaboration has been consistently shown to be an essential element of what it means to be human (Ehin, 1998; Izgar, 2009; Rees & Johnson, 2007; Schlichte, Yssel, & Merbler, 2005). Ancestors who could not get along well with others were probably less able to survive, and as we saw in the stress-reward endorphin cycle, collaboration leading to survival may have produced in us the pleasurable pattern of an endorphin release: working together feels good (Johnson, 2003; Pembroke, 2008). Given this natural tendency toward collaboration, isolationist practices in schools are not only poorly designed with regard to systemic performance, they go against our natural human instincts as well.

Collaboration Reduces Stress, Fear, and Feelings of Isolation

Attempting to overcome generational academic failure isn't work that can be handled alone. Many teachers toil away with feelings of stress and isolation in the face of these challenges, fearing their efforts are futile. The recognition that these problems are too big for anyone acting alone is in fact what leads to the stress and isolation. Collaboration helps reduce this stress and gives hope that even the most burdensome problems can be resolved.

Collaboration Reveals Problems

Schools today often mistakenly assume that collaboration solves all problems, but a case can be made that initially it reveals more problems than it solves. A dysfunctional family that finally seeks therapy is likely to have a rough time in the first few months, as years of neglected issues rise to the surface. The same is true in schools where collaboration has been ignored for generations. Collaboration might force people who don't like each other very much to work together. Personality conflicts, prejudices, and disconnects with professional aspirations and goals may be revealed for the first time. None of these problems is solved initially by collaboration, but continuing a pattern of isolation is not the answer, either. Even highly functional schools that become adroit at collaboration will continue to reveal more problems and challenges *because* of it—but highly functioning schools get better at resolving them.

Frederick Taylor and Scientific Management

While other professions are continuously transformed by fierce competition and technological innovation, education evolves at a snail's pace. One reason schools haven't changed as much as businesses in the last hundred years is that despite our challenges, schools never went *out* of business. While entire industries rose and fell and reinvented themselves, schools continued chugging along, with relatively little change (Heckman & Montera, 2009).

When schools became consolidated in the early 1900s, their organizational structure was based on Frederick Taylor's scientific management theory (Eisner, 2002; Gray, 1993), which was developed to facilitate the management of large industrialized structures like factories and mills. Taylorism allowed the production of cars and other goods in a cheap, consistent, and efficient manner and created systems for managing large numbers of people who were often performing boring and redundant tasks—and for a time these approaches worked (Jones, 2000). Managers established strict and predictable job descriptions and rigid hierarchy and used time studies and bells to move people through the system (Taylor, 1947).

A cardinal principal of Taylorism was isolation. It was believed that when people worked together productivity was diminished and that workers toiling alone were less distracted (Taylor, 1911; Peaucelle, 2000). In the first half of the twentieth century, our educational system subscribed to this same ethic of isolationism. Classrooms were separated by thick plaster walls, which divided the work of teachers and ensured the quiet and solitude that were thought necessary to promote learning. When looking at these older buildings, it's also clear that underlying their design was the assumption that there was little need for teachers to come together except when the bell rang signaling lunch.

It's no wonder that we have to fight so hard today to develop strategies around collaboration: despite our natural human tendency to work together, our schools were designed to keep us apart.

Collaboration Allows for Legitimate Shared Leadership

When considering the generations of teachers and other staff members who have worked in relative isolation, it's disheartening to imagine the number of great leaders who might have emerged from among them but couldn't. We tend to have a rather myopic view of leadership and expect leaders to stand up, stand out, and lead with a roar. In fact, leadership is often quiet—thoughtful and reflective people can be the best leaders and have a huge impact on a culture when given the chance to do so. Collaboration allows for the emergence of leadership from people with a variety of perspectives regarding the very meaning of learning and leadership.

Collaboration Calls on Us to Shape and Reshape Goals and Objectives

Over the years, many school leaders have presented poor decisions from the top down with clarity and high expectations. Although there are certainly occasions when decisions must be made in this way, thoughtful learning leaders instead cocreate a vision or goal and whenever possible give collaborative teams the responsibility for identifying strategies for reaching it (Chen, Tjosvold, & Liu, 2006). In turn, teams bring clarity to visions and goals, informing the process while delivering a product. The best collaborative teams, in fact, have a direct hand in constructing a vision or goal, accountability for pursuing it, and license along the way to improve upon and reshape it in a way that doesn't detract from its original intent. Of course, this can be very tricky and requires a high level of connection, a commitment to deep learning, and a tolerance for the occasional misstep along the way. This level of participation allows collaborative teams to be inspired and empowered as well as learning focused.

Common Collaborative Patterns in School

In this section, in order to gain perspective on the state of collaboration in learning organizations today, we introduce collaborative patterns often found in schools.

Schools That Don't Collaborate

The first pattern is the absence of collaboration. These schools continue to work in ways that would make Frederick Taylor proud. Except for structured staff and department meetings, teachers get their orders and toil alone. These schools have meetings just to keep the group honest, calling out the lowest common denominator of staff performance. Agenda items might include time spent correcting the entire staff for behaviors exhibited by a small minority, rather than aiming in the direction of inspired performance.

Schools That "Meet" but Don't Collaborate

Some schools have begun to establish consistent meeting structures and made gestures toward creating a learning community but haven't found a way to meaningfully collaborate. They may have a number of traditional leaders in the organization who continue to dominate the agenda and regard collaboration as simply a new opportunity to get people together to continue to promulgate their views and opinions. This interpretation of collaboration can actually put an organization further behind. A group of highly motivated, thoughtful professionals working in complete isolation might make some progress by accident. However, groups that meet all the time but don't collaborate wind up diminishing their time and energy. In many respects, this is the worst-case scenario.

Schools That Try to Collaborate But Don't Know Why

Teams need to know why they are being asked to collaborate. Unfortunately, too many schools have adopted collaboration as an end in itself. Schools don't exist to collaborate; they collaborate to meet their most essential goals and objectives. Leaders that lose sight of this think somehow they've passed the finish line by simply getting people to meet consistently in teams. If groups don't have a clear idea of why they are meeting, it's likely that they aren't taking learning to the deepest levels. The most effective groups often have a purpose or goal up front as well as a date certain by which the group will be disbanded. Sometimes knowing that a group isn't going to be together forever creates a greater sense of urgency and improves the learning.

Schools That Collaborate About the Wrong Things

Meaningful and sustained collaboration, unfortunately, hasn't been the focus of leadership and management structures for very long. It's not surprising, then, that a number of schools collaborate around the wrong objectives or collaborate when it's completely unnecessary. For example, attempting to collaborate in a large group on editing a piece of writing can be a frustrating process, since it is difficult to integrate all the ideas and opinions into one piece of coherent prose. Some school improvement teams, for example, will spend time "collaborating" for an hour in May over the paper order for next fall, putting off a discussion regarding opening-day professional development that would certainly have a much deeper impact on the school's progress. Many school leaders have yet to develop a sense of timing and perspective when determining if a large or small group is needed to make a decision, or if one person—such as the principal—can make the call.

Schools That Collaborate Around Low-Stakes Outcomes

Some school staff who are new to collaboration feel a bit uneasy about the jolt to their sensibilities when a number of personalities come together. When we ask teachers to collaborate, we must acknowledge fully that alternative opinions, beliefs, and ideals are going to come into conflict, and that will create tension at times. Certainly, if you believe in collaboration, this opportunity to grow is well worth it. However, in the face of this discomfort, some schools decide to collaborate primarily around low-stakes outcomes. Instead of being honest with themselves about grade-level expectations or collaborating on assessment strategies, they collaborate on issues requiring only minimal effort and have very little chance of stirring controversy.

Schools That Remember to Collaborate but Forget Individual Learning

Some schools with great intentions have become absolutely obsessed with collaboration yet have neglected individual learning. Collaboration should inform individual learning at a very deep level. An inspired and focused team that meets regularly can offer stimulating exchanges that allow the participants to reflect later on the collaborative experience and come back more prepared than ever for the next round of dialogue and collaboration. That next round won't be meaningful, though, if team members do not take the time to reflect on their individual learning. In the best organizations, individual and team learning are continuously supported and are demonstrated in organizational practices.

Schools Whose Collaborative Strategies Inspire Deep Learning

When groups can collaborate in a meaningful and thoughtful way using strategies that promote learning, there is very little they cannot accomplish. The great victories in pre-K–12 education in the last fifty years were almost never initiated by a governor's signature on a bill or a board of education mandate. They typically came about when a motivated group of staff members at the building level decided they were going to make the mental and emotional investment to change their world. By coming together in a spirited and collaborative fashion, they did.

Solutions in Action: Learning-Centered Collaboration Strategies

The learning-centered collaboration strategies that follow not only promote the power of people working together but also support the individual and collective learning capacities that deserve deeper levels of stimulation in schools today.

Step One: Adopt Collaboration as a Corporate Nonnegotiable

The brain pays more attention to actions than words. Actions can drive learning and often create a deeper connection with our values and belief systems than anything we can say (Martin, McCrone, Bower, & Dindyal, 2005; O'Reilly & Frank, 2006). Many organizations today talk about the power of collaboration and make collaboration available but don't act on it—they don't mandate it. Schools have a tendency to be more permissive in this area than other professions.

During the 1990s, when many corporations invested in reengineering strategies, they made collaboration nonnegotiable. The Owens Corning Headquarters in Toledo, Ohio, abandoned its multistoried hierarchical corporate office and constructed a flat headquarters that reflected the collaborative leadership values and beliefs they were attempting to promote. Throughout the organization, unassigned collaboration spaces were made available to provide opportunities for good ideas and thoughtful people to come together spontaneously; the company recognized this was going to be an important ethic in the organization.

After the company made this intellectual and economic investment, people weren't allowed to opt out of collaboration—it became an essential nonnegotiable. Schools serious about collaborative learning must do the same.

Step Two: Support Both Formal and Spontaneous Collaboration

At the new Owens Corning headquarters, no one "owned" the flexible meeting space. Even though most schools today don't have this type of unassigned space, teachers and other staff members should be encouraged to break into spontaneous collaboration whenever they can. By using staff meetings for impromptu collaboration or creating small teams for short-term projects, principals can promote the notion that spontaneous and natural collaboration strongly supports the learning process—even in organizations that are already invested in becoming learning communities.

Step Three: Continually Ask, "Is Collaboration Necessary?"

Thoughtful learning leaders are encouraged to ask this question anytime an important decision is made or thoughtful learning is about to take place. Obviously, when considering essential school improvement outcomes, the answer is almost always a resounding yes. Collaboration regarding important goals and objectives is absolutely essential to creating a deep level of buy-in and connectivity with the learning agenda.

In any school, there are also multiple occasions where decisions regarding collaboration are made to some degree on the spur of the moment. Over the summer, a principal may be contacted by a book vendor who wants to make a key change to materials ordered for fall; the principal may have to decide whether to authorize the change on his or her own or try to find others in the middle of vacation to look at the issue. There is no formula for coming up with a right answer.

In practice, many schools waste time collaborating on issues that are unimportant. If we are fatigued and overwhelmed, we may choose to collaborate over issues that do not require deeper levels of stimulation and challenge. Collaborative teams may need to live with relatively minor decisions made by an individual in isolation and instead use their time together to pursue initiatives that really matter.

Step Four: Create Empowered and Accountable Teams

When collaborative teams are formed, it is essential that they be given as much empowerment, recognition, and accountability as possible. This means there must be clarity going into the work regarding exactly what they are allowed to do, to whom they are accountable, and how public their results will be. In their haste to implement collaboration, many schools have asked teachers to come together regarding essential goals and objectives but have withheld from them serious decision-making authority. When a team of highly trained adults has little authority, they typically feel little sense of accountability. Some teams welcome the empowerment but seek to shed the accountability, and that should be discouraged. Teams need to be thoughtful about embracing both.

Finally, recognition is extremely important with a collaborative team. Promoting its work and recognizing its accomplishments will help stimulate a more profound commitment to the organization and to the concept of collaboration itself.

Step Five: Establish a Collaborative Skill-Building Team

The larger the organization, the more difficult it is to manage the collaboration process. This is why, wherever possible, thoughtful learning leaders should create a skill-building team whose goal is to manage and evaluate the collaboration process itself. This group, which is usually composed of teachers, administrators, and other staff, should not be regarded as the one with decision-making authority. Instead, its charge is to support skill development using the collaboration process. This team can resolve conflicts before they result in long-term dysfunction or diminished learning capacity, evaluate professional development and skill-building opportunities that might assist teams, create a sense of accountability, and inspire collaboration in ways that support organizational learning. Finally, a skill-building team can be a reminder to the entire school that collaboration is a key value and is nonnegotiable.

The goal of collaborative skill building might also be assigned for a year to a team that leads the creation of the professional development agenda or to a school improvement steering committee.

Step Six: Organize Collaboration Strategies

To organize the work of collaborators effectively, it's essential to discuss goals and evaluate the original justification for the group. Some groups collaborate with the intention of rigorously maintaining their individual autonomy, using the opportunity to collaborate in order to simply build up their own resistance to any type of collaborative approach! Other groups use their time together to reshape their perspectives and come up with a more unified front on change. Asking if the group is necessary and specifically pointing out what it is trying to achieve saves time and effort in the end.

Schools that have established values for the entire organization must include those values as a component of collaborative work as well. If values have not been established, they should be discussed. What does the group stand for? What does it value? What is it willing to do, or not do, in pursuit of its goals?

Successful collaborative teams also need a sense of clarity regarding the role of each team member and the value he or she intends to bring. One team member may be excellent at disaggregating data or seeing an opposing point of view. Other team members may have skill at using technology or establishing collaborative relationships beyond the building. A thoughtful discussion regarding what a new teacher, veteran teacher, or teacher moving from another level can bring to a team will enhance the contributions of all team members and allow them to frame their participation in a way that is of greatest help.

Being thoughtful regarding the size of teams is an important and underdiscussed aspect of collaboration. The size of the team affects the degree to which members can work together in an authentic and deeply interconnected way. Teams must be sized in a way that is appropriate to the learning challenge at hand. Tackling school improvement may require a team composed of the entire school, with subgroups for discrete continuous improvement functions. To some degree, this is a matter of trial and error, but in general, teams that are too large often lack the intimacy and connectivity necessary to access deeper levels of creativity and connection (Lowry, Roberts, Dean, & Marakas, 2009; Guimera, Uzzi, Spiro, & Amaral, 2005).

Finally, establishing a firm set of ground rules can help a collaborative team be much more effective. These rules could include, for example, how often the team will meet and what variables will drive the need for the group to come together. The team may need to identify the amount of "air time" any team member is permitted to use during the meetings. Strategies should also be established regarding how the agenda is developed and who has the authority to coordinate the use of collaboration time.

Step Seven: Use Thoughtful Debate to Improve Learning

Some view the presentation of alternative perspectives as an act of war; others feel that by debating an issue we reflect on the content more effectively than by simply listening passively. Even when a group is in total agreement regarding an issue, it can be helpful to assign several members of the team the job of coming up with alternative positions to help the team consider its nuances. Some issues may require days, weeks, and months of debate in order to make a decision that may affect the school's future over a long period of time. Debating issues—not people— has the potential to create an environment that is more stimulating without making group members feel they are being attacked or criticized. Debate can also stimulate deep learning. Collaborative teams need to get comfortable with this strategy.

Step Eight: Demand a Diversity of Perspectives Within the Collaborative Process

Thoughtful learning leaders need to move beyond the notion that diversity is something to be tolerated or accepted. What we know now about learning tells us that we must *insist* upon it. Without a diversity of perspectives, we run the risk of evaluating issues myopically. Of course, a group that is very clear about its beliefs and focused on its goals is not likely to change course to any great extent as a result. The introduction of alternative viewpoints may simply serve the valuable purpose of reinforcing the rightness of the existing objectives. With groups that are relatively homogeneous, it is important to actively seek outside opinions, even if the groups have to obtain input from individuals beyond the school district. This takes extra effort, but it leads to deeper levels of learning.

Step Nine: Get Comfortable With Mistakes and Allow Others to Find Their Voice

Collaboration can keep groups from making serious mistakes. With diverse perspectives around the table, challenges that might have gone unrecognized before can be seen and dealt with. However, it's essential to recognize that teams, too, will make mistakes—and teams themselves have to be prepared for this eventuality. Forceful leaders often become prominent because they make good decisions and have clear notions about what needs to be done. Collaboration allows more people to develop this skill, but teams will have to trust that the result is worth some trial and error along the way.

Step Ten: Enjoy, and Celebrate!

Even though the work of schools is serious and important, teams can still associate their work with joy and fun. Difficult challenges handled together can provide interesting and stimulating opportunities for a thoughtful group of leaders. Laughing together makes the time we spend at work—which represents a huge portion of our lives—more enjoyable. At the most basic physiological level, we have learned that collaboration can stimulate a pleasurable response (Waelti, Dickinson, & Schultz, 2001). When we come together, we feel more comfortable—the brain rewards us for assembling as a tribe. When we laugh, even more endorphins are released.

As we have seen, celebration and ceremony also help us to retain and build our memories. When we celebrate groups for their efforts and when teams themselves relive their learning through ceremony—even by just getting together and reflecting in an enjoyable way, they stimulate deep levels of learning.

Through collaboration, school staff members can interact with each of the strategies in this book in a unique way: all of the strategies can be applied more effectively by teams that meet regularly. A thoughtful debate enriched by diverse perspectives is bound to produce a better result. Although schools should be mindful of when a decision is best left to an individual, in most cases collaborative work teams that are empowered and accountable can meet challenges more comprehensively, and more enjoyably, than individuals acting alone.

CHAPTER 10

Conclusion

Learning leadership is a relevant framework for both principals and teachers because of where we have been and where we are headed. Expectations for academic performance will continue to arch upward, coupled with the ongoing hope that we can simultaneously meet an array of profound social challenges. We are supposed to teach everyone, and with the splendor of diversity comes the task of accurately identifying and meeting everyone's needs. Distractions due to the speed of technology will continue to plague us as our individual and collective mental bandwidth remains relatively static, while supercomputers learn to process the world faster and faster. Our jobs will continue to become increasingly specialized and technical, requiring the continued emergence of leadership that is less and less defined by position.

Leadership, learning, and change are a single force today. We will be able to meet the needs of the present and future only by using what we know about learning and strategically applying that knowledge so that each of us can directly connect with more of our own learning potential. Coming in a time that requires so much more of us, learning leadership will allow us to work smarter and do more during this short period we have together—improving our capacity to collaborate, learn, and evolve.

It is of paramount importance for learning leaders to remember that learning starts with emotion. By applying the steps of strategic emotional focus, leaders can establish a much more thoughtful learning culture; the actions required by this process can stimulate profound and essential emotions that are often ignored in schools. By specifically calling out emotions like courage and determination and then identifying actions that support those mindsets, learning leaders will become professionally stronger, open themselves to greater possibilities, and stimulate their learning more deeply than ever before.

As we saw earlier in this book, fight or flight, even in small amounts, can lead to stress, anger, loneliness, and other emotional states that can reduce our capacity to focus on a learning agenda. Fear materializes in learning organizations whenever we are faced with change. In an effort to minimize its influence, thoughtful learning leaders must deal with it directly. The change, analysis, and reframing strategy allows groups working in thoughtful learning organizations to directly confront fear and keep it from hindering their progress. This strategy also allows schools to think about change systemically and realistically and to fully acknowledge factors that awaken fear without letting them inhibit progress.

In exploring our often ambivalent relationship with stress, we examined how to interrupt the stress-reward cycle in order to keep stress from overwhelming us. By having control of our emotions, keeping fear in perspective, and minimizing the creeping influence of stress, teams of learning leaders will find themselves better prepared to deal with their challenges and commitments.

We examined a much used but seldom analyzed term in relationship to leadership: *vision*. As important as it is, precious little time has been spent on ascertaining the actual steps leaders must take to create a vision. This text focused on vision's relationship to individual and organizational learning. The protocol we recommend for strategic vision construction is vital to learning leaders who wish to move away from what are often vague and perhaps romanticized notions of what it means to establish a vision. Leaders must keep in mind that establishing a collective vision is a very complex task, closely aligned with what we know about learning. Systems for developing vision that have a greater connection to mechanisms for learning will improve our capacity to see where we are going and identify with greater precision the steps needed to get there.

This text identified tools for making the learning environment more accessible for thoughtful learning leaders. We explored the use of inquiry and the degree to which strategically established inquiry pursuits can stimulate learning and help us take what might simply be an emotional connection to an idea or vision and add to it clarity and specificity.

By directly calling out the need to establish a defined learning culture, learning leaders were reminded of a number of environmental factors that can stimulate deep learning for the adults in school. Being aware of the power of context and consolidation and the rigorous and direct pursuit of relaxed alertness will pay dividends for learning leaders who bring these strategies to bear on their challenges.

En route to driving deeper levels of learning, we also revealed some of the limits and untapped potential of memory. A better understanding of how our memory systems work and how many learning focal points we can think about at any given time empowers learning leaders to be more disciplined in their learning agendas. Identifying strategies for deep organizational learning and strategically defining a school's focal points enables us not only to learn more but also to embed that learning for years to come.

Finally, we examined in depth the power of collaboration and its influence on learning. Learning leaders today must go beyond the steps we took, as recently as a few years ago, when we thought that simply by putting people together in groups we were overcoming generations of isolation. In overcoming the legacy of Taylorism and the deliberate isolation it called for, schools must be equally deliberate in analyzing the steps they take to create cultures of collaboration.

Teacher leaders who apply learning leadership to their craft can potentially make deeper connections with their colleagues, stimulate the force of organic leadership that exists in their organization, and make a significant difference in the lives of the students they serve. Principals who are learning leaders can support teacher leaders in this work by making management decisions that sustain these approaches to leadership.

The challenges ahead in pre-K–12 education are profound. Children will continue to struggle, and communities will need every ounce of intellectual and emotional ingenuity that is available to them. Schools throughout the rest of this century will transfer and reinvent our culture, and finding better ways to do so will require a stronger approach to working together and leading change. Learning leadership honors and supports the efforts of the brave, spirit-driven, loving, thoughtful people who go to work each day in our schools to meet this challenge.

References

Abedi, J., & Gandara, P. (2006). Performance of English language learners as a subgroup in large-scale assessment: Interaction of research and policy. *Educational Measurement: Issues and Practice, 25*(4), 36–46.

Achterman, D., & Loertscher, D. V. (2008). Where in the role are you anyway? *CSLA Journal, 31*(2), 10–13.

Adelman, H. S., & Taylor, L. (2007). Systemic change for school improvement. *Journal of Educational & Psychological Consultation, 17*(1), 55–77.

Adolphs, R., Baron-Cohen, S., & Tranel, D. (2002). Impaired recognition of social emotions following amygdala damage. *Journal of Cognitive Neuroscience, 14*(8), 1264–1274.

Amitai, Y., & Connors, B. W. (1995). Intrinsic physiology and morphology of single neurons in neocortex. In E. G. Jones & I. T. Diamond (Eds.), *The barrel cortex of rodents* (pp. 299–332). New York: Plenum Press.

Anbu, J. (2008). Developing intelligent feelings. *Nursing Standard, 22*(9), 52.

Anderson, D. R. (2007). A neuroscience of children and media? *Journal of Children and Media, 1*(1), 77–85.

Angliss, C. (2008). How your health affects your job. *Office Pro, 68*(7), 14–17.

Arievitch, I. M., & Haenen, J. P. (2005). Connecting sociocultural theory and educational practice: Galperin's approach. *Educational Psychologist, 40*(3), 155–165.

Awartani, M., Whitman, C. V., & Gordon, J. (2008). Developing instruments to capture young people's perceptions of how school as a learning environment affects their well-being. *European Journal of Education, 43*(1), 51–70.

Baas, M., DeDrue, C., & Nijstad, B. (2008). A meta-analysis of 25 years of mood-creativity research: Hedonic tone, activation, or regulatory focus? *Psychological Bulletin, 134*(6), 779–806.

Baker, W., Trofimovich, P., Flege, J. E., Mack, M., & Halter, R. (2008). Child-adult differences in second language phonological learning: The role of cross language similarity. *Language and Speech, 51*(4), 317–342.

Barnett, M. M. (2006). Does it hurt to know the worst?—Psychological morbidity, information preferences and understanding of prognosis in patients with advanced cancer. *Psycho-Oncology, 15*(1), 44–55.

Barra, J., Bray, A., Sahni, V., Golding, J., & Gresty, M. (2005). Increasing cognitive load with increasing balance challenge: Recipe for catastrophe. *Experimental Brain Research, 174*(4), 734–735.

Barrett, E. (2007). Experiential learning in practice as research: Context, method, knowledge. *Journal of Visual Art Practice, 6*(2), 115–124.

Bass, B., & Avolio, B. (1988). Transformational leadership: Charisma and beyond. In J. Hunt, B. Baliga, H. Dachler, & C. Shriesheim (Eds.), *Emerging leadership vistas* (pp. 29–49). Toronto: D.C. Heath.

Bateson, P., Barker, D., Clutton-Brock, T., Debal, D., D'Udine, B., Foley, R. A., et al. (2004). Developmental plasticity and human health. *Nature, 430*(6998), 419–421.

Battro, A., Fischer, K., & Lena, P. J. (2008). *The educated brain.* New York: Cambridge University Press.

Baumgartner, T., Valko, L., Esslen, M., & Jancke, L. (2006). Neural correlate of spatial presence in an arousing and noninteractive virtual reality: An EEG and psychophysiology study. *CyberPsychology and Behavior, 9*(1), 30–45.

Bayer, R. (2008). TV affects children's cognitive development. *Canadian Journal of Health and Nutrition, 314,* 52.

Belleville, S., Rouleau, N., Van der Linden, M., & Collette, F. (2003). Effect of manipulation and irrelevant noise on working memory capacity of patients with Alzheimer's dementia. *Neuropsychology, 17*(1), 69–81.

Belmonte, A., & Cranston, N. (2009). The religious dimension of lay leadership in Catholic schools: Preserving Catholic culture in an era of change. *Catholic Education, 12*(3), 294–319.

Bergan, J. F., Ro, P., Ro, D., & Knudsen, E. I. (2005). Hunting increases adaptive auditory map plasticity in adult barn owls. *Journal of Neuroscience, 25,* 9816–9820.

Berkman, L. F., & Glass, X. (2000). Social integration, social networks, social support, and health. In L. F. Berkman and I. Kawachi (Eds.), *Social epidemiology* (pp. 137–173). New York: Oxford University Press.

Bernstein, G. A., Bernat, D. H., Davis, A. A., & Layne, A. E. (2008). Symptom presentation and classroom functioning in a nonclinical sample of children with social phobia. *Depression and Anxiety, 25*(9), 752–760.

Berridge, K. C., & Kringelbach, M. L. (2008). Affective neuroscience of pleasure: Reward in humans and animals. *Psychopharmacology, 199,* 457–480.

Billington, J., & Baron-Cohen, S. (2007). Savant memory for digits in a case of synaesthesia and Asperger Syndrome is related to hyperactivity in the lateral prefrontal cortex. *Neurocase (Psychology Press), 13*(5–6), 311–319.

Blanchard, D. C., Griebel, G., & Blanchard, R. J. (2001). Mouse defensive behaviors: Pharmacological and behavioral assays for anxiety and panic. *Neuroscience and Biobehavioral Reviews, 25,* 205–218.

Borja, R. R. (2005). State support varies widely. *Education Week, 24*(35), 18–24.

Bosco, F. (2007). Emotions that build networks: Geographies of human rights movements in Argentina and beyond. *Journal of Economic and Social Geography, 98*(5), 545–563.

Braine, M. E. (2009). The role of the hypothalamus, Part 1: The regulation of temperature and hunger. *British Journal of Neuroscience Nursing, 5*(2), 66–72.

Brehmer, Y., Straube, B., Stoll, G., Li, S. C., von Oertzen, T., Muller, V., & Lindenburger, U. (2008). Comparing memory skill maintenance across the life span: Preservation in adults, increase in children. *Psychology and Aging, 23*(2), 227–238.

Bronkhorst, A. W. (2000). The cocktail party phenomenon: A review of research on speech intelligibility in multiple-talker conditions. *Acustica, 86,* 694–703.

Brungart, D. S., & Simpson, B. D. (2007). Effect of target-masker similarity on across-ear interference in a dichotic cocktail-party listening task. *Journal of the Acoustical Society of America, 122*(3), 1724–1734.

Burns, J. M. (1978). *Leadership.* New York: Harper & Row.

Busche, G. R., & Kassam, A. F. (2005). When is appreciative inquiry transformational? *Journal of Applied Behavioral Science, 41*(2), 161–181.

Bushman, B. J., Baumeister, R. F., & Phillips, C. M. (2001). Do people aggress to improve their mood? Catharsis beliefs, affect regulation opportunity, and aggressive responding. *Journal of Personality and Social Psychology, 81,* 17–32.

Butler, E. A., Egloff, B., Wilhelm, F., Smith, N., Erickson, E., & Gross, J. (2003). The social consequences of expressive suppression. *Emotion, 3*(1), 48–67.

Butler, E. A., Lee, T., & Gross, J. (2007). Emotion regulation and culture: Are the social consequences of emotion suppression culture-specific? *Emotion, 7*(1), 30–48.

Butterworth, B. (2005). The development of arithmetical abilities. *Journal of Child Psychology & Psychiatry, 46*(1), 3–18.

Cacioppo, J. T., Hughes, M. E. Waite, L. J., Hawkley, L. C., & Thristed, R. A. (2006). Loneliness as a specific risk factor for depressive symptoms: Cross-sectional and longitudinal analyses. *Psychology and Aging, 21*(1), 140–151.

Cahill, L. (2000, January 19). *Emotions and memory.* Speech given at the Learning Brain Expo, San Diego, CA.

Cahill, L., Prins, B., Weber, M., & McGaugh, J. L. (1994). β-Adrenergic activation and memory for emotional events. *Nature, 371*(6499), 702–704.

Caine, R. N., Caine, G., McClintic, C., & Klimek, K. (2005). *12 brain/mind learning principles in action.* Thousand Oaks, CA: Corwin Press.

Campbell, J. (2003). Goals 2000: A modest proposal for reform. *Research for Educational Reform, 8*(2), 40–46.

Campbell, J. L., & Bigger, A. S. (2008). Cleanliness and learning in higher education. *Executive Housekeeping Today, 30*(9), 6–22.

Carrillat, F. A., d'Astrous, A., & Colbert, F. (2008). The effectiveness of art venue sponsorship: An attribution perspective. *Journal of Sponsorship, 1*(3), 274–285.

Carver, C. S. (1998). Resilience and thriving: Issues, models, and linkages. *Journal of Social Issues, 54,* 245–266.

Chapman, C., Ramondt, L., & Smiley, G. (2005). Strong community, deep learning: Exploring the link. *Innovations in Education and Teaching International, 42*(3), 217–230.

Chen, G., & Kanfer, R. (2006). Toward a systems theory of motivated behavior in work teams. In B. M. Staw (Ed.), *Research in Organizational Behavior*, vol. 27 (pp. 223–267). Oxford, UK: Elsevier.

Chen, G., Tjosvold, D., & Liu, C. (2006). Cooperative goals, leader people and productivity values: Their contribution to top management teams in China. *Journal of Management Studies, 43*(5), 1177–1200.

Cherry, E. C. (1953). Some experiments on the recognition of speech, with one and with two ears. *Journal of Acoustical Society of America, 25,* 975–979.

Christakis, D. A., Zimmerman, F. J., DiGiuseppe, D. L., & McCarty, C. (2004). Early television exposure and subsequent attentional problems in children. *Pediatrics, 113,* 708–713.

Cobb, C. G. (2003). *From quality to business excellence: A systems approach to management.* Milwaukee, WI: American Society for Quality.

Cohen, D. A., & Robertson, E. M. (2007). Motor sequence consolidation: Constrained by critical time windows or competing components. *Experimental Brain Research, 177*(4), 440–446.

Cohen, G., & Conway, M. A. (2008). *Memory in the real world.* New York: Psychology Press.

Compton, R. J. (2003). The interface between emotion and attention: A review of evidence from psychology and neuroscience. *Behavioral and Cognitive Neuroscience, 2,* 115–129.

Cooperrider, D. L., Whitney, D., & Stavros, J. M. (2003). *Appreciative inquiry handbook* (2nd ed.). San Francisco: Berrett-Koehler.

Coulter, C. M. (2006). Appreciating the best of our past to navigate the future. In *Currents and Convergence, Navigating the Rivers of Change* (pp. 26–31). Paper presented at the Association of College and Research Libraries Twelfth National Conference, April 7–10, 2005, Minneapolis, MN.

Cowan, N., Morey, C., & Chen, Z. (2007). The legend of the magical number seven. In S. Della Sala, *Tall tales about the mind and brain* (pp. 45–59). New York: Oxford University Press.

Darr, W., & Johns, G. (2008). Work strain, health, and absenteeism: A meta-analysis. *Journal of Occupational Health Psychology, 13*(4), 293–318.

Davidoff, J. (2000). *Brain and behavior.* New York: Routledge.

Davies, R. S., & Osguthorpe, R. T. (2003). Reflecting on learner intent. *Reflective Practice, 4*(3), 303–315.

Day, C. (2000). Beyond transformational leadership. *Educational Leadership, 57*(7), 56–60.

Day, G. S. (2003). Creating a superior customer-relating capability. *MIT Sloan Management Review, 44*(3), 77–82.

Dehaene, S. (2005). Evolution of human cortical circuits for reading and arithmetic: The "neuronal recycling" hypothesis. In S. Dehaene, J. R. Duhamel, M. D. Hauser, & G. Rizzolatti (Eds.), *From monkey brain to human brain* (pp. 133–157). Cambridge, Massachusetts: MIT Press.

DePaulo, B. M., & Kashy, D. A. (1998). Everyday lies in close and casual relationships. *Journal of Personality and Social Psychology, 74,* 63–79.

de Rivera, J., Kurrien, R., & Olsen, N. (2007). The emotional climate of nations and their culture of peace. *Journal of Social Sciences, 63*(2), 255–271.

Dillon, D. G., Ritchey, M., Johnson, B. D., & LaBar, K. S. (2007). Dissociable effects of conscious emotion regulation strategies on explicit and implicit memory. *Emotion, 7*(2), 354–365.

Dochy, F., Segers, M., & Buehl, M. M. (1999). The relation between assessment practices and outcomes of studies: The case of research on prior knowledge. *Review of Educational Research, 69,* 145–186.

DuFour, R. (2004). What is a professional learning community? *Educational Leadership, 61*(8), 6–11.

DuFour, R., DuFour, R., & Eaker, R. (2008). *Revisiting professional learning communities at work.* Bloomington, IN: Solution Tree Press.

Dziegielewski, S. F., Jacinto, G. A., Laudaio, A., & Legg-Rodriguez, L. (2003). Humor. *International Journal of Mental Health, 32*(3), 74–90.

Ebersohn, L., Maree, K., & Maree, J. G. (2006). Demonstrating resilience in an HIV and AIDS context: An emotional intelligence perspective. *Gifted Education International, 22*(1), 14–30.

Egorov, A. V., Unsicker, K., & von Bohlen, O. (2006). Muscarinic control of graded persistent activity in lateral amygdala neurons. *European Journal of Neuroscience, 24*(11), 3183–3194.

Ehin, C. (1998). Fostering both sides of human nature—the foundation for collaborative relationships. *Business Horizons, 41*(3), 15–26.

Eisner, E. W. (2002). *The educational imagination.* Columbus, OH: Prentice Hall.

Fadul, J. A. (2007). Resonant teaching: Prolonging the half-life of the learning process. *International Journal of Learning, 14*(1), 27–31.

Fanselow, M. S., & Lester, L. S. (1988). A functional behavioristic approach to aversively motivated behavior: Predatory imminence as a determinant of topography of defensive behavior. In R. Bolles & M. Beecher (Eds.), *Evolution and learning* (pp. 185–211). Hillsdale, NJ: Erlbaum.

Fenker, D., & Schutze, H. (2008). Learning by surprise. *Scientific American Mind, 19*(6), 47.

Foley, M. S., Foley, H. J., Scheye, R., & Bonacci, A. M. (2007). Remember more than meets the eye: A study of memory confusions about incomplete visual information. *Memory, 15*(6), 616–633.

Fox, E., Russo, R., Bowles, R. J., & Dutton, K. (2001). Do threatening stimuli draw or hold visual attention in sub-clinical anxiety? *Journal of Experimental Psychology, 130,* 681–700.

Franklin, J. (2005, June). Mental mileage: How teachers are putting brain research to use. *Education Update, 47*(6), 1–7.

Freeman, W. J. (2004). How and why brains create meaning from sensory information. *International Journal of Bifurcation & Chaos, 14,* 513–530.

Freitas, A. L., & Downey, G. (1998). Resilience: A dynamic perspective. *International Journal of Behavioral Development, 22*(2), 263–285.

Frese, M. (2008). The word is out: We need an active performance concept for modern workplaces. *Industrial & Organizational Psychology, 1*(1), 67–69.

Friedel, K. S., Cortina, J., Turner, C., & Midgley, C. (2007). Achievement goals, efficacy beliefs and coping strategies in mathematics: The roles of perceived parent and teacher goal emphases. *Contemporary Educational Psychology, 32*(3), 434–458.

Friedman, W. J. (2007). The development of temporal metamemory. *Child Development, 78*(5), 1472–1491.

Fullan, M. (2006). The future of educational change: System thinkers in action. *Journal of Educational Change, 7,* 113–122.

Gadzella, B., Masten, W., & Zascavage, V. (2009). Differences among three groups of men on stress and learning processes. *Individual Differences Research, 7*(1), 29–39.

Garner, M., Mogg, K., & Bradley, B. (2006). Orienting and maintenance of gaze to facial expressions in social anxiety. *Journal of Abnormal Psychology, 115*(4), 760–770.

Gathercole, S. E., Alloway, T. P., Willis, C., & Adams, A. M. (2006). Working memory in children with reading disabilities. *Journal of Experimental Psychology, 83*(3), 265–281.

Giles, C., & Hargreaves, A. (2006). The sustainability of innovative schools as learning organizations and professional learning communities during standardization reform. *Educational Administration Quarterly, 42,* 124–156.

Goetz, T., Frenzel, A. C., Pekrun, R., Hall, N. C., & Ludtke, O. (2007). Between- and within-domain relations of students' academic emotions. *Journal of Educational Psychology, 99,* 715–733.

Goldsborough, R. (2009). A New Year's resolution: Battling information overload. *Public Relations Tactics, 16*(1), 15.

Goleman, D., & Boyatzis, R. (2008). Social intelligence and the biology of leadership. *Harvard Business Review, 86*(9), 74–81.

Gopnik, A., Meltzoff, A., & Kuhl, P. (1999). *The scientist in the crib: Minds, brains, and how children learn.* New York: William Morrow.

Graetz, K. A., & Goliber, M. J. (2002). Designing collaborative learning places: Psychological foundations and new frontiers. *New Directions for Teaching and Learning, 92,* 13–22.

Gray, K. (1993). Why we will lose: Taylorism in America's high schools. *Phi Delta Kappan, 74*(5), 370–375.

Greenly, L. W. (1997). The phenomenon of pain. Part 5: Sensory and motor control systems. *Chiropractic Technique, 9*(1), 49.

Gregory, G. H., & Parry, T. (2006). *Designing brain-compatible learning* (3rd ed.). Thousand Oaks, CA: Corwin Press.

Gross, J. J. (1998). Antecedent- and response-focused emotion regulation: Divergent consequences for experience, expression, and physiology. *Journal of Personality and Social Psychology, 2,* 224–237.

Gross, J. J., & John, O. P. (2002). *Individual differences in two emotion regulation processes: Implications for affect, relationships, and well-being.* Manuscript submitted for publication.

Gross, J. J., & Levenson, R. W. (1997). Hiding feelings: The acute effects of inhibiting negative and positive emotion. *Journal of Abnormal Psychology, 106,* 95–103.

Gross, L. (2006). When seeing is misleading: Clutter leads to high-confidence errors. *PLoS Biology, 4*(3), 301–302.

Gross, P. (2009). Socializing secondary-level student teachers: Is this happening in your school? *Clearing House, 82*(4), 177–182.

Guerard, K., & Tremblay, S. (2008). Revisiting evidence for modularity and functional equivalence across verbal and spatial domains in memory. *Journal of Experimental Psychology: Learning, Memory and Cognition, 34*(3), 556–569.

Guimera, R., Uzzi, B., Spiro, J., & Amaral, L. A. (2005). Team assembly mechanisms determine collaboration network structure and team performance. *Science, 308*(5722), 697–702.

Gura, T. (2008). I'll do it tomorrow. *Scientific Mind, 19*(6), 27–33.

Gygax, P. M., Wagner-Egger, P., Parris, B., Seiler, R., & Hauert, C. A. (2008). A psycholinguistic investigation of football players' mental representations of game situations: Does expertise count? *Swiss Journal of Psychology, 67*(2), 85–95.

Hall, M. G. (2007). Voting in state supreme court elections: Competition and context as democratic incentives. *Journal of Politics, 69*(4), 1147–1159.

Hallinger, P. (2003). Leading educational change: Reflections on the practice of instructional and transformational leadership. *Cambridge Journal of Education, 33*(3), 239–351.

Hallinger, P., & Heck, R. (2002). What do you call people with visions? Vision, mission and goals in school leadership and improvement. In K. Leithwood & P. Hallinger (Eds.), *Second international handbook of educational leadership and administration* (pp. 9–40). The Netherlands: Kluwer.

Halm, M. A. (2009). Clinical evidence review. Relaxation: A self-care healing modality reduces harmful effects of anxiety. *American Journal of Critical Care, 18*(2), 169–172.

Harris, C. R. (2001). Cardiovascular responses or embarrassment and effects or emotional suppression in a social setting. *Journal of Personality and Social Psychology, 81,* 886–897.

Hastings, L. T., & Hastings, R. P. (2008). Psychological variables as correlates of adjustment in mothers of children with intellectual disabilities: Cross-sectional and longitudinal relationships. *Journal of Intellectual Disability Research, 52*(1), 37–48.

Hayes, A., & Freyd, J. (2002). Representational momentum when attention is divided. *Visual Cognition, 9*(1/2), 8–27.

Heckman, P. E., & Montera, V. L. (2009). School reform: The flatworm in a flat world—from entropy to renewal through indigenous invention. *Teachers College Record, 111*(5), 1328–1351.

Hess, J. (Director). (2004). *Napoleon Dynamite* [Motion picture]. United States: Fox Searchlight Pictures.

Hickey, D. T., & Zuiker, S. J. (2005). Engaged participation: A sociocultural model of motivation with implications for educational assessment. *Educational Assessment, 10*(3), 277–305.

Hirsch, C. R., Hayes, S., & Mathews, A. (2009). Looking on the bright side: Accessing benign meanings reduces worry. *Journal of Abnormal Psychology, 118*(1), 44–54.

Horwitz, S., & Horwitz, I. (2007). The effects of team diversity on team outcomes. *Journal of Management, 33,* 987–1015.

Hughes, J. (Director). (1986). *Ferris Bueller's day off* [Motion picture]. United States: Paramount Pictures.

Hunt, M. G., Milonova, M., & Moshier, S. (2009). Catastrophizing the consequences of gastrointestinal symptoms in irritable bowel syndrome. *Journal of Cognitive Psychotherapy, 23*(2), 160–173.

Hutton, F. (2005). Risky business: Gender, drug dealing and risk. *Addiction Research & Theory, 13*(6), 545–554.

Immordino-Yang, M. H., & Damasio, A. (2007). We feel, therefore we learn: The relevance of affective and social neuroscience to education. *Mind, Brain and Education, 1*(1), 3–10.

Izac, S. M. (2006). Basic anatomy and physiology of sleep. *American Journal of Electroneurodiagnostic Technology, 46*(1), 18–38.

Izgar, H. (2009). An investigation of depression and loneliness among school principals. *Educational Sciences: Theory and Practice, 9*(1), 247–258.

Jacobs, G. (2003). *The ancestral mind: Reclaim the power.* New York: Penguin Group.

Jennings, J. R., & van der Molen, M. W. (2005). Preparation for speeded action as a psychophysiological concept. *Psychological Bulletin, 131*(3), 434–459.

Johnson, B. (2003). Teacher collaboration: good for some, not so good for others. *Educational Studies, 29*(4),

Jones, O. (2000). Scientific management, culture and control: A first-hand account of Taylorism in practice. *Human Relations, 53*(5), 631–653.

Kaliprasad, M. (2006). The human factor II: Creating a high performance culture in an organization. *Cost Engineering, 48*(6), 27–34.

Kangasharju, H., & Nikko, T. (2009). Emotions in organizations. *Journal of Business Communication, 46*(1), 100–119.

Kaplan, S., Bradley, J. C., Luchman, J. N., & Haynes, D. (2009). On the role of positive and negative affectivity in job performance: A meta-analytic investigation. *Journal of Applied Psychology, 94*(1), 162–176.

Karakose, T. (2008). The perceptions of primary school teachers on principal cultural leadership behaviors. *Educational Sciences, 8*(2), 569–579.

Kennedy, T. J. (2006). Language learning and its impact on the brain: Connecting language learning with the mind through content-based instruction. *Foreign Language Annals, 39*(3), 471–486.

Kersten, A. W., & Earles, J. L. (2001). Less really is more for adults learning a miniature artificial language. *Journal of Memory and Language, 44*, 250–273.

Kimmerle, J., Moskaliuk, J., & Cress, U. (2008). Individual learning and collaborative knowledge building with shared digital artifacts. *Proceedings of World Academy of Science, Engineering and Technology, 36*, 719–726.

Klein, K., & Bratton, K. (2007). The costs of suppressing stressful memories. *Cognition and Emotion, 21*(7), 1496–1512.

Koenig, H., McCullough, M., & Larson, D. (2001). *Handbook of religion and health*. New York: Oxford University Press.

Koenig, S., & Mecklinger, A. (2008). Electrophysiological correlates of encoding and retrieving emotional events. *Emotion, 8*(2), 162–173.

Kokinov, B. (1999). Dynamics and automaticity of context: A cognitive modeling approach. In P. Bouquet, L. Serafini, P. Brezillon, M. Benerecetti, & F. Castellani (Eds.), *Modeling and using context* (pp. 200–213). *Lecture notes in artificial intelligence, 1688.* Berlin: Springer.

Kouzes, J. M., Posner, B. Z. (2009). To lead, create a shared vision. *Harvard Business Review, 87*(1), 20–21.

Kringelbach, M. L. (2004). Food for thought: Hedonic experience beyond homeostasis in the human brain. *Neuroscience, 126,* 807–819.

Kringelbach, M. L. (2008). *The pleasure center: Trust your animal instincts.* New York: Oxford University Press.

Kuh, G. D. (2007). What student engagement data tell us about college readiness. *Peer Review, 9*(1), 4–8.

Kujala, J. K., Pammer, P. L. Cornelissen, P., Roebroeck, A. Formisano, E., & Salmelin, R. (2007). Phase coupling in a cerebro-cerebellar network at 8–13 Hz during reading. *Cerebral Cortex, 17,* 1476–1485.

Kumar, A., Rakitin, B., Nambisan, R., Habeck, C., & Stern, Y. (2008). The response-signal method reveals age-related changes in object working memory. *Psychology and Aging, 23*(2), 215–239.

LaBar, K. S. (2007). Beyond fear: Emotional memory mechanisms in the human brain. *Current Directions in Psychological Science, 16*(4), 173–177.

Lamontagne, A. D., Keegel, T., Louie, A., Ostry, A., & Landsbergis, P. A. (2007). A systematic review of the job-stress intervention evaluation literature, 1990–2005. *International Journal of Occupational and Environmental Health, 13,* 268–280.

Larsen, R. L. (2000). Toward a science of mood regulation. *Psychological Inquiry, 11,* 129–142.

Lazarus, R. (1998). The costs and benefits of denial. In R. S. Lazarus (Ed.), *Fifty years of research and theory* (pp. 227–251). New York: Lawrence Erlbaum Associates.

Lee, D., & Birdsong Sabatino, K. (1998). Evaluating guided reflection: A U.S. case study. *International Journal of Training and Development, 2*(3), 162–170.

Lee, J. G., & Thorson, E. (2008). The impact of celebrity-product incongruence on the effectiveness of product endorsement. *Journal of Advertising Research, 48*(3), 433–449.

Lee, K., Ee, L., & Ng, S. F. (2009). The contributions of working memory and executive functioning to problem representation and solution generation in algebraic word problems. *Journal of Educational Psychology, 101*(2), 373–387.

Lees, A., Mogg, K., & Bradley, B. (2005). Health anxiety sensitivity, and attentional biases for pictorial and linguistic health threat cues. *Cognition and Emotion, 19*(3), 453–462.

Levenson, R. W. (2003). *Autonomic specificity and emotion.* In R. J. Davidson, H. H. Goldsmith, and K. R. Scherer (Eds.), *Handbook of effective science* (pp. 212–224). New York: Oxford University Press.

Lipton, B. H. (2008). *The biology of belief.* New York: Hay House.

Liu, R. L., Shih, M. J., & Kao, Y. F. (2001). Adaptive exception monitoring agents for management by exceptions. *Applied Artificial Intelligence, 15*(4), 397–418.

London, M. (1997). Overcoming career barriers: A model of cognitive and emotional processes for realistic appraisal and constructive coping. *Journal of Career Development, 24*(1), 25–38.

Lowry, P. B., Roberts, T. L., Dean, D. L., & Marakas, G. (2009). Toward building self-sustaining groups in PCR-based tasks through implicit coordination: The case of heuristic evaluation. *Journal of the Association for Information Systems, 10*(3), 170–195.

Ludick, M., Alexander, D., & Carmichael, T. (2007). Vicarious traumatisation: Secondary traumatic stress levels in claims workers in the short-term insurance industry in South Africa. *Problems and Perspectives in Management, 5*(3), 99–110.

Lupien, S. L., & Schramek, T. E. (2006). The differential effects of stress on memory consolidation and retrieval: A potential involvement of reconsolidation? Theoretical comment on Beckner et al. *Behavioral Neuroscience, 120*(3), 735–738.

MacDonald, K. B. (2008). Effortful control, explicit processing, and the regulation of human evolved predispositions. *Psychological Review, 115*(4), 1012–1031.

Machado, C., Kazama, A. M., & Bachevalier, J. (2009). Impact of amygdala, orbital frontal, or hippocampal lesions on threat avoidance and emotional reactivity in nonhuman primates. *Emotion, 9*(2), 147–163.

Margolis, H. (2005). Resolving struggling learners' homework difficulties: Working with elementary school learners and parents. *Preventing School Failure, 50*(1), 5–12.

Marquardt, M. J. (2004). *Optimizing the power of action learning.* Palo Alto, CA: Davies Black Publishing.

Marsh, E. J. (2007). Retelling is not the same as recalling: Implications for memory. *Current Directions in Psychological Science, 16*(1), 16–20.

Martin, T., McCrone, S., Bower, M., & Dindyal, J. (2005). The interplay of teacher and student actions in the teaching and learning of geometric proof. *Educational Studies in Mathematics, 60*(1), 95–124.

Mate, G. (2004). Suppressing our emotions harm physical and mental health. *Alive: Canadian Journal of Health and Nutrition, 258,* 28–29.

Mathews, A., & MacLeod, C. (1994). Cognitive approaches to emotion and emotional disorders. *Annual Review of Psychology, 45,* 25–50.

McAllister, C. L., Thomas, T. L., Wilson, P. C., & Green, B. L. (2009). Root shock revisited: Perspectives of early Head Start mothers on community and policy environments and their effects on child heath, development and school readiness. *American Journal of Public Health, 99*(2), 205–210.

McElree, B. (2001). Working memory and the focus of attention. *Journal of Experimental Psychology: Learning, Memory, and Cognition, 27,* 817–835.

McEwen, B. S. (1998). Protective and damaging effects of stress mediators. *N. Engl. J. Med. 338:* 171–179.

McEwen, B. S. (2004). Protection and damage from acute and chronic stress: Allostasis and allostatic overload and relevance to the pathophysiology of psychiatric disorders. *Annuals of the New York Academy of Science, 1032,* 1-7.

McEwen, B., & Lasley, E. (2003). Allostatic load: When protection gives way to damage. *Advances, 19*(1), 28–33.

Meltzoff, A. N. (2007). The "like me" framework for recognizing and becoming an intentional agent. *Acta Psychologica, 124,* 26–43.

Merrill, M. D., & Gilbert, C. G. (2008). Effective peer interaction in a problem-centered instructional strategy. *Distance Education, 29*(2), 199–207.

Merritt, R. (2008). Classroom environment (pp. 1-16). Great Neck Publishing. Accessed from Research Starters—Education database on September 2, 2009.

Mineka, S., & Ohman, A. (2002). Phobias and preparedness: The selective, automatic, and encapsulated nature of fear. *Biological Psychiatry, 52*(10), 927–937.

Miyashita, Y. (2004). Cognitive memory: Cellular and network machineries and their top-down control. *Science, 306*(5695), 435–440.

Mogg, K., & Bradley, B. P. (1998). A cognitive-motivational analysis of anxiety. *Behaviour Research and Therapy, 35,* 297–303.

Mohan, K., Peng, X, & Ramesh, B. (2008). Improving the change-management process. *Communications of the ACM, 51*(5), 59–64.

Moldovan, A. R., Onac, I. A., Vantu, M., Szentagotai, A., & Onac, I. (2009). Emotional distress, pain catastrophizing and expectancies in patients with low back pain. *Journal of Cognitive and Behavioral Psychotherapies, 9*(1), 83–93.

Moss, J., Kotovsky, K., & Cagan, J. (2006). The role of functionality in the mental representation of engineering students: Some differences in the early stages of expertise. *Cognitive Science, 30*(1), 65–93.

MSNBC. (2007, June 12). Rudy's 11 . . . uh 12 commitments. FirstRead on MSNBC online. Accessed at http://firstread.msnbc.msn.com/archive/2007/06/12/223446.aspx on April 30, 2009.

Murphy, J. M. (2007). Breakfast and learning: An updated review. *Current Nutrition and Food Science, 3*(1), 3–36.

Myers, D. G. (2000). Hope and happiness. In E. P. Seligman and J. Gillham (Eds.), *The science of optimism and hope* (pp. 232–336). Philadelphia: Templeton Foundation Press.

Nairne, J. S. (2002). Remembering over the short-term: The case against the standard model. *Annual Review of Psychology, 53*(1), 53–82.

Nolen-Hoeksema, S. (1991). Responses to depression and their effects on the duration of depressive episodes. *Journal of Abnormal Psychology, 100,* 569–582.

Noyce, J. (2003, August 22). Help employees manage stress to prevent absenteeism, errors. *Minneapolis/St. Paul Business Journal.* Accessed at www.bizjournals.com/twincities/stories/2003/08/25/smallb2.html?page=1 on May 1, 2009.

Nworie, J., & Haughton, N. (2008). Good intentions and unanticipated effects: The unintended consequences of the application of technology in teaching and learning environments. *TechTrends: Linking Research and Practice to Improve Learning, 52*(5), 52–58.

Oathes, D. J., & Ray, W. J. (2008). Dissociative tendencies and facilitated emotional processing. *Emotion, 8*(5), 653–661.

Oberauer, K. (2002). Access to information in working memory: Exploring the focus of attention. *Journal of Experimental Psychology: Learning, Memory, and Cognition, 28,* 411–421.

Oberauer, K., & Bialkova, S. (2009). Accessing information in working memory: Can the focus of attention grasp two elements at the same time? *Journal of Experimental Psychology: General, 138*(1), 64–87.

Ocasio, L. (2005). Schools: City kids. *Ford Foundation Report, 36*(1), 13–14.

Olsson, G. M., Marild, S., Alm, J., Brodin, U., Rydelius, P., & Marcus, C. (2008). The Adolescent Adjustment Profile (AAP) in comparisons of patients with obesity, phenylketonuria or neurobehavioural disorders. *Nordic Journal of Psychiatry, 62*(1), 66–76.

O'Reilly, R. C., & Frank, M. J. (2006). Making working memory work: A computational model of learning in the prefrontal cortex and basal ganglia. *Neural Computation, 18*(2), 283–328.

Osinsky, R., Reuter, M., Kupper, Y., Schmitz, A., Kozyra, E., Alexander, N., & Hennig, J. (2008). Variation in the serotonin transporter gene modulates selective attention to threat. *Emotion, 8*(4), 584–588.

Palmer, S., & Puri, A. (2006). *Coping with stress at university.* Thousand Oaks, CA: Sage.

Panda, Y. (2008). Emotional intelligence and perceived stress. *Journal of Organizational Behavior, 7*(3), 13–16.

Paz, R., Pelletier, J., Bauer, E., & Pare, D. (2006). Emotional enhancement of memory via amygdala-driven facilitation of rhinal interactions. *Neuroscience, 9*(10), 1321–1329.

Peaucelle, J. (2000). From Taylorism to post-Taylorism simultaneously pursuing several management objectives. *Journal of Organizational Change Management, 13*(5), 452.

Pekrun, R., Goetz, T., Titz, W., & Perry, R. P. (2002). Positive emotions in education. In E. Frydenberg (Ed.), *Beyond coping: Meeting goals, visions, and challenges* (pp. 149–174). Oxford, England: Elsevier.

Pekrun, R., Maier, M., & Elliot, A. (2009). Achievement goals and achievement emotions: Testing a model of their joint relations with academic performance. *Journal of Educational Psychology, 101*(1), 115–135.

Pembroke, G. (2008). Helper's high. *Canadian Journal of Health and Nutrition, 304,* 128–129.

Peters, K. R., Ray, L., Smith, V., & Smith, C. (2008). Changes in the density of stage 2 sleep spindles following motor learning in young and older adults. *Journal of Sleep Research, 17*(1), 23–33.

Petrecca, L. (2007, March 21). We should be feeling very sleepy, considering flood of sleep aids. *USA Today.* Accessed at www.usatoday.com/money/advertising/adtrack/2007-03-11-rozerem_N.htm on May 12, 2009.

Preskill, H. S., & Catsambas, T. T. (2006). *Reframing evaluation through appreciative inquiry.* Thousand Oaks, CA: Sage.

Preuss, G. A. (2003). High performance work systems and organizational outcomes: The mediating role of information quality. *Industrial and Labor Relations Review, 56*(4), 590–560.

Primary Review. (2008). *Literacy Today, 55,* 11.

Rathi, N., & Rastogi, R. (2008). Effect of emotional intelligence on occupational self-efficacy. *ICFAI Journal of Organizational Behavior, 7*(2), 46–56.

Reason, C., & Reason, L. (2007). Asking the right questions. *Educational Leadership, 65*(1), 36–40.

Rees, D., & Johnson, R. (2007). All together now? Staff views and experiences of a pre-qualifying interprofessional curriculum. *Journal of Interprofessional Care, 21*(5), 543–555.

Ressler, K. J., & Mayberg, H. S. (2007). Targeting abnormal neural circuits in mood and anxiety disorders: From the laboratory to the clinic. *Nature Neuroscience, 10*(9), 1116–1124.

Richards, J. M., & Gross, J. J. (1999). Composure at any cost? The cognitive consequences of emotion suppression. *Personality and Social Psychology Bulletin, 25,* 1033–1044.

Richards, J. M., & Gross, J. J. (2000). Emotion regulation and memory: The cognitive costs of keeping one's cool. *Journal of Personality and Social Psychology, 79,* 410–424.

Robertson, E. M. (2009). From creation to consolidation: A novel framework for memory processing. *PLoSBiology, 7*(1), 19–28.

Rogers, D. L., & Babinski, L. M. (2002). From isolation to conversation: Supporting new teachers' development. Albany, NY: State University of New York Press.

Romero, L. M., & Butler, L. K. (2007). Endocrinology of stress. *International Journal of Comparative Psychology, 20,* 89–95.

Roxhorough, I. (2000). Organizational innovation: Lessons from military organizations. *Sociological Forum, 15*(2), 367–372.

Rozanski, A., Blumenthal, J. A., & Kaplan, J. (1999). Impact of psychological factors on the pathogenesis of cardiovascular disease and implications for therapy. *Circulation: Journal of the American Heart Association, 99,* 2192–2217. Accessed at http://circ.ahajournals.org/cgi/reprint/99/16/2192 on July 7, 2009.

Rydeen, J., & Erickson, P. (2002). A positive environment. *American School and University, 75,* 36–38.

Sapolsky, R. (1998). *Why zebras don't get ulcers: An updated guide to stress, stress-related diseases, and coping.* New York: Freeman.

Schlichte, J. L., Yssel, N., & Merbler, J. (2005). Pathways to burnout: Case studies in teacher isolation and alienation. *Preventing School Failure, 50*(1), 35–40.

Scott, R. B., & Dienes, Z. (2008). The conscious, the unconscious, and familiarity. *Journal of Experimental Psychology, 34*(5), 1264–1288.

Sebrant, U. (2008). The impact of emotion and power relations on workplace learning. *Studies in the Education of Adults, 40*(2), 192–206.

Seeman, T. (2001). How do others get under our skin? In C. D. Ryff & B. H. Singer (Eds.), *Emotion, social relationships and health* (pp. 189–210). New York: Oxford University Press.

Seidl, W. (2009). Empower staff to tackle stress. *Occupational Health, 61*(3), 9.

Sen, S. (2008). Executives and the stress factor. *Journal of Soft Skills, 2*(1), 39–44.

Seung-Schik, Y., Hu, P. T., Gujar, N., Jolesz, F. A., & Walker, M. P. (2007). A deficit in the ability to form new human memories without sleep. *Nature Neuroscience, 10*(3), 385–392.

Shu-Shen, S. (2008). The relation of self-determination and achievement goals to Taiwanese eighth graders' behavioral and emotional engagement in schoolwork. *Elementary School Journal, 108*(4), 313–324.

Smallwood, J., Fitzgerald, A., Miles, L. K., & Phillips, L. H. (2009). Shifting moods, wandering minds: Negative moods lead the mind to wander. *Emotion, 9*(2), 271–276.

Smeltz, A. (2007, November 14). Prescription-drug abuse escalates. *McClatchy-Tribune Business News.* Accessed at http://proquest. umi.com.ezproxy.apollolibrary.com/pqdweb?did=138252393 1&sid=2&Fmt=3&clientId=13118&RQT=309&VName=PQD on May 12, 2009.

Soo-Young, K., & Jong-Jin, K. (2006). Influence of light fluctuation on occupant visual perception. *Building and Environment, 42*(8), 2888–2899.

Sornson, R. (2005). *Creating classrooms where teachers love to teach and students love to learn.* Golden, CO: Love and Logic Press.

Sorrell, J. M. (2008). Remembering: Forget about forgetting and train your brain instead. *Journal of Psychosocial Nursing and Mental Health Services, 46*(9), 25–27.

Sprinkle, R., Hunt, S., Simonds, C., & Comandena, M. (2006). Fear in the classroom: An examination of the teachers' use of fear appeals and students' learning outcomes. *Communication Education, 55*(4), 389–402.

Steffen, P. R., & Masters, K. S. (2005). *Annals of Behavioral Medicine, 20*(3), 217–224.

Stone, C. A., & Lane, S. (2003). Consequences of a state accountability program: Examining relationships between school performance gains and teacher, student, and school variables. *Applied Measurement in Education, 16*(1), 1–26.

Stout, M. (2007). *The paranoia switch: How terror rewires our brains and reshapes our behavior and how we can reclaim our courage.* New York: Sarah Crichton Books.

Strong-Wilson, T. (2006). Bringing memory forward: A method for engaging teachers in reflective practice on narrative and memory. *Reflective Practice, 7*(1), 101–113.

Sullivan, M. J., Lynch, M. E., Clark, J. A., Mankovsky, T., & Sawynok, J. (2008). Catastrophizing and treatment outcome: differential impact on response to placebo and active treatment outcome. *Contemporary Hypnosis, 25*(3/4), 129–140.

Tapola, A., & Niemivirta, M. (2008). The role of achievement goal orientations in students' perceptions of and preferences for classroom environment. *British Journal of Educational Psychology, 78,* 291–312.

Taylor, F. (1911). *Scientific management.* New York: Harper & Row.

Taylor, F. W. (1947). *The principles of scientific management.* New York: Harper & Row.

Thompson, N., & Wheeler, J. P. (2008). Learning environment: Creating and implementing a safe, supportive learning environment. *Journal of Family and Consumer Sciences, 26*(2), 33–43.

Tice, D. M., & Bratslavsky, E. (2000). Giving in to feeling good: The place of emotion regulation in the context of general self-control. *Psychological Inquiry, 11,* 149–159.

Tice, D. M., Bratslavsky, E., & Baumeister, R. F. (2001). Emotional distress regulation takes precedence over impulse control: If you feel bad, do it! *Journal of Personality and Social Psychology, 80*(1), 53–67.

Tiede, H. L., & Leboe, J. P. (2009). Metamemory judgments and the benefits of repeated study: Improving recall predictions through the activation of appropriate knowledge. *Journal of Experimental Psychology: Learning, Memory, and Cognition, 35*(3), 822–828.

Tompkins, J. (2005). Don't outsource the relationship, *Industrial Engineer, 37*(11), 28–33.

Tronson, N. C., & Taylor, J. R. (2007). Molecular mechanisms of memory reconsolidation. *Nature Reviews Neuroscience, 8*(4), 262–266.

Uchino, B., Cacioppo, J. T., & Kiekolt-Glaser, J. K. (1996). The relationship between social support and physiological processes: A review with emphasis in underlying mechanisms and implications for health. *Psychological Bulletin, 119,* 488–531.

Upitis, R. (2004). School architecture and complexity. *Complicity: An International Journal of Complexity and Education, 1*(1), 19–38.

Van den Berg, A. E., & ter Heijne, M. (2005). Fear versus fascination: An exploration of emotional responses to natural threats. *Journal of Environmental Psychology, 25,* 261–272.

Vandewalle, G., Gais, S., Schabus, M., Balteau, E., Carrier, J., Darsaud, A., et al. (2007). Wavelength-dependent modulation of brain responses to a working memory task by daytime light exposure. *Cerebral Cortex, 17*(12), 2788–2804.

VanRullen, R., Guyonneau, R., & Thorpe, S. J. (2005). Spike times make sense. *Trends in Neurosciences, 28,* 1–4.

Verduyn, P., Delvaux, E., Van Coillie, H., Tuerlinckx, F., & Van Mechelen, I. (2009). Predicting the duration of emotional experience: Two experience sampling studies. *Emotion, 9*(1), 83–91.

Vinton, K. E. (1989). Humor in the workplace: It's more than telling jokes. *Small Group Behavior, 20*(2), 151–166.

Vohs, K. D., Baumeister, R. F., Schmeichel, B. J., Twenge, J. M., Nelson, N. M., & Tice, D. M. (2008). Making choices impairs subsequent self-control: A limited resource account of decision-making, self-regulation, and active initiative. *Personality and Social Psychology, 94*(5), 883–898.

Waelti, P., Dickinson, A., & Schultz, W. (2001). Dopamine responses comply with basic assumptions of formal learning theory. *Nature, 412,* 43–48.

Ward, A. (2008). Beyond the instructional mode: Creating a holding environment for learning about the use of self. *Journal of Social Work Practice, 22*(1), 67–83.

Weisinger, H. (1998). *Emotional intelligence at work.* San Francisco: Jossey-Bass.

Whitney, D. K., & Trosten-Bloom (2003). *The power of appreciative inquiry: A practical guide to positive change.* San Francisco: Berrett-Koehler.

Williams, J. M., Barnhofer, T., Crane, C., Hermans, D., Raes, F., Watkins, E., et al. (2007). Autobiographical memory specificity and emotional disorder. *Psychological Bulletin, 133*(1), 122–148.

Williams, J. M. G., Chan, S., Crane, C., Barnhofer, T., Eade, J., & Healy, H. (2006). Retrieval of autobiographical memories: The mechanisms and consequences of truncated search. *Cognition and Emotion, 20,* 351–382.

Wolfe, P. (2001). *Brain matters: Translating research into classroom practice.* Alexandria, VA: Association for Supervision and Curriculum Development.

Wood, G. E., Norris, E. H, Waters, E., & Stoldt, J. (2008). Chronic immobilization stress alters aspects of emotionality and associative learning in the rat. *Behavioral Neuroscience, 122*(2), 282–292.

Yang, J., & Mossholder, K.W. (2004). Decoupling task and relationship conflict: The role of intragroup emotional processing. *Journal of Organizational Behavior, 25*(5), 589–605.

Yap, C., & Richardson, R. (2007). The ontogeny of fear-potentiated startle: Effects of earlier-acquired fear memories. *Behavioral Neuroscience, 121*(5), 1053–1062.

Yates, J. W., Chalmer, B., St. James, P., Follansbee, M, & McKegney, F. P. (1981). Religion in patients with advanced cancer. *Medical and Pediatric Oncology, 9,* 121–128.

Young, J. (2009). Enhancing emergent literacy potential for young children. *Australian Journal of Language and Literacy, 32*(2), 163–180.

Zak, P., Borja, K., Kurzban, R., & Matzner, W. (2005). The neuroeconomics of distrust: Sex differences in behavior and physiology. *American Economic Review, 95*(2), 360–363.

Zech, E. (2000). *The effects of the communication of emotional experiences.* Unpublished doctoral dissertation. University of Louvain, Belgium.

Zheng, G., & Tonnelier, A. (2008). Chaotic solutions in the quadratic integrate-and-fire neuron with adaptation. *Cognitive Neurodynamics.* Accessed at www.inrialpes.fr/bipop/people/tonnelier/ chaosQIF.pdf on March 15, 2009.

Index

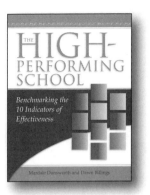

The Collaborative Administrator
Austin Buffum, Cassandra Erkens, Charles Hinman, Susan Huff, Lillie G. Jessie, Terri L. Martin, Mike Mattos, Anthony Muhammad, Peter Noonan, Geri Parscale, Eric Twadell, Jay Westover, and Kenneth C. Williams
Foreword by Dr. Robert Eaker
In a culture of shared leadership, the administrator's role is more important than ever. This book addresses your toughest challenges with practical strategies and inspiring insight. **BKF256**

The High-Performing School: Benchmarking the 10 Indicators of Effectiveness
Mardale Dunsworth and Dawn Billings
Become a high-performing school by implementing the on-site school review—a cooperative venture between an external review team and a school's administrators, teachers, and students. **BKF294**

District Leadership That Works: Striking the Right Balance
Robert J. Marzano and Timothy Waters
Learn strategies for creating district-defined goals while giving building-level staff the stylistic freedom to respond quickly and effectively to student failure. **BKF314**

Transforming School Culture: How to Overcome Staff Division
Anthony Muhammad
Busy administrators will appreciate this quick read packed with immediate, accessible strategies for transforming toxic school cultures into healthy environments conducive to change. **BKF281**

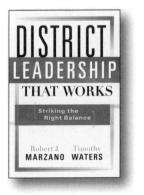